W9-AMU-242

TALIESIN

POEMS

Taliesin

POEMS

Introduction
and
English
translation
by

MEIRION PENNAR

ISBN 0947992243

Published by
LLANERCH ENTERPRISES
in 1988

CONTENTS

Introduction

The poems

ILLUSTRATIONS

Instead of modern drawings designed to illustrate scenes in the poems, which may have upset the reader's imagination, we have selected several examples of late-Celtic, Romano-British, Celtic-Christian art, and artefacts, with which to embellish the text. They are listed below against their page numbers.

Note: The manuscript-facsimile and Welsh text is taken from Dr. J. G. Evans' "Book of Taliesin."

INTRODUCTION

Who was Taliesin?

Taliesin has always attracted the attention of antiquarians and literators since the time of his rediscovery in the ancient Book of Taliesin, in the eighteenth century, by the likes of Turner, and Ieuan Fardd. He was admired for the power and directness of his most celebrated poem to Urien, namely the Battle of Argoed Llwyfain. It was primitive and raw to them. But the Taliesin of other poems, not addressed to Urien, has been a fascination of the lovers of Celtic literature. This Taliesin is the bard supreme, who self-consciously towers above the rest; the seer and shape-shifter whose work epitomises the notion of reincarnation which supposedly forms the crux of Celtic religious belief. The poet of such lines as these:

> Eil gweith ym rithad
> bum glas gleissad,
> bum ki, bum hyd,
> bum iwrch ymynyd.

> The second time I was charmed
> I was a silver salmon,
> I was a hound, I was a stag,
> I was a mountain buck.

Twentieth-century scholarship, however, has distinguished very clearly between these two Taliesins. John Morris-Jones and Ifor Williams realized that the poems to Urien were the work of a professional bard, a master of the short eulogy, while the others were poems written in the persona of a poet with supernatural powers and a propensity for the occult akin to the Taliesin of the mediaeval legend entitled 'Chwedl Taliesin' as it is repro-

7

duced in the Myvyrian Archiology of 1870, and which can be read in English by having recourse to the Guest translation of the Mabinogion.

The Book of Taliesin (Pen. 2 in the National Library, a late thirteenth-century manuscript) is an interesting collection of poetry, some of which is connected with neither the eulogist nor the legend. It was finally redacted in the eleventh century as an act of love by the last in a possible series of monks involved in the mediaeval cult of Taliesin. Latin interpolations, such as the well-known 'lauda, laudate, Jesu,' and several religious poems contained in the manuscript betray further that monkish involvement in the compilation of the book. 'Marwnad y Fil Feib' is an invocation of the saints of the ages, while some of the poems which have secular titles and whose material may originally have had pre-Christian roots, are now reworked or recreated with a devotional Christian bias.

Even though the poems are 'edited' compositions from different periods, and by an admixture of secular and religious authors, what is astounding is that there is no tampering with the poems of Taliesin the eulogist. Of the Book of Taliesin, the poems now widely accepted on Ifor Williams' final recommendation (in his book entitled 'Canu Taliesin' [1961], for which there is an English version by Caerwyn Williams, published by the Dublin Institute for Advanced Studies), are those to Urien, the elegy on his son Owain, and the poems to Cynan Garwyn and to Gwallawg. There does not seem to be any need to change this list of the most likely poems of the historical Taliesin. The other poems in the book are unlikely to be the work of Taliesin the bard; they have been attributed to him, very obviously in some cases where

8

the poet as actor names himself, and by impli-
cation in others.

Taliesin the eulogist lived in the sixth century.
He may well have come from Powys, witness the
poem to the Powys lord Cynan Garwyn. But his
poetic activity as a eulogist was centered mainly
in Northern Britain, Cumberland, Westmorland and
Galloway in particular, which then formed the
Brythonic or North Cymric kingdom of Rheged.
There he sang the praises of Urien the lord of
Rheged and his son Owain, and of Gwallawg, the
lord of Elfed near present-day Leeds. Whether
these poems in the Book of Taliesin actually re-
present the work of Taliesin the sixth-century
bard, or are the adapted version of a later age,
has been recently discussed. What was the Bryth-
onic language like by the end of the sixth century?
Had it lost its terminations? Kenneth Jackson
seems to think so. If not, then the poems of Tal-
iesin would have been rather different, and they
would have been emended to their present form
at a later date. Problems abound with this too.
How could a poem reasonably survive those lin-
guistic changes of the sixth century without losing
its shape? In other words, the well defined form
and structure of Taliesin's poetry, with a primitive
Welsh rhyming system, is yet another proof that
Brythonic lost its terminations very early on and
very quickly, and that by the time Taliesin was
composing, Cymric or Cumbric had already been
born. Taliesin and Aneirin must have been among
the first to have composed in it. They did so with
panache. Hence their enduring fame.

Where was Rheged?

According to the maturest reflections of Ifor Williams, Rheged straddled the area around the Solway Firth, 'Merin Rheged' as it was called in Taliesin's day. It included the northernmost area of Cumberland as far as Carlisle, and stretched towards Stranraer and northwards towards Ayr (in Cymric, Aeron). Its eastern limits are a matter for conjecture, for Urien had extended his domain by conquest to include Catraeth or Catterick, the site of that famous and tragic battle so unforgettably recorded by Aneirin a generation or so later. Thus the sway of Urien Rheged was quite extensive and may well have stretched down as far as beyond Wensleydale, where a battle was fought against the English which ended in a great triumph for the North Cymric tribe.

The name Rheged has been associated with Rochdale and Dunragit. But could Urien's kingdom have stretched from Lancashire to Stranraer? Part of Urien's kingdom was called Llwyfenydd which Ifor Williams would have us connect with the river Lyvennet in Westmorland. He is named as the lord of Erch, which Ifor Williams links with the river Ark which flows into the Swale near Catterick. Urien was a great warrior, and he was instrumental in the second half of the sixth century in stemming the ever-encroaching Saxon. Perhaps he was the lord of Erch through conquest. There is mention of a possible cattle-raid on Manaw (if Maw is emended) which is the Brythonic kingdom centered on Edinburgh. The actual kingdom of Rheged must have had its nucleus around Carlisle, Caer Liwelydd in Welsh, mentioned by Hywel ab Owain Gwynedd, the famous twelfth-century poet, in conjunction with a journey undertaken by him to Rheged. Idon (re-established as part of the text by Ifor Williams) is most assuredly the river Eden, flowing from Appleby to Carlisle.

Gwallawg, another lord, who inspired the praise of Taliesin, ruled over Elfed, the name of which is preserved in Elmet near Leeds. The lands of Cynan Garwyn, for which one poem by Taliesin survives, included the later Welsh kingdom of Powys and parts of present-day Shropshire and Lancashire as well. Thus mobility between these different lands of the Cymry (which is derived from 'Combrogi' meaning 'inhabitants of the same territory') meant that Taliesin did not think twice about leaving Powys for the North and thence from the Solway Firth to Leeds. Even if the language was not exactly the same, the language and craft of the poet was.

Taliesin the Poet.

It is definite, on the poet's own avowal, in a poem to Urien, that Taliesin did not come from Rheged. In the poem to the people of Rheged he says clearly "although I am not one of yours." If not from Rheged, then from where? Perhaps his poem to Cynan Garwyn gives us a clue. He may have sung the praises of Cynan before making his way to the North, to the land of Urien. Cynan was the king of Powys. He was a king of considerable stature and power and as such made an impression on Taliesin. He is the forager of the lands of Brycheiniawg; he led a campaign against the men of the Wye valley, and the men of Gwent. He is "the harrasser of Cornwall." Again the remarkable extent of the mobility of the Brythons, now Cymry, is apparent.

The age of Taliesin was the final age of Brythonic power and ascendancy. It was an age of resurgence, striving, and hope and success against the Saxon tide. Not since Arthur had their spirit been so high. Within a generation the attempt of the Gododdin to prevent the English from spreading further was cruelly aborted at the battle of Catraeth around 600 A.D. Soon Powys was to recede into present-day Wales because of the ever-encroaching Mercians. In the time of Taliesin, however, it bordered on the extended kingdom of Urien beyond Lancaster and stretched eastwards towards Elmet near Leeds. Cynan Garwyn was an energetic and forceful leader raiding Wye-land, Gwent, and Cornwall. He was successful in plunder-mongering, and was rich. His generosity knew no bounds. One has the impression that he was magnanimous to the point of ostentation. Taliesin says that he got from him a hundred horses, a hundred robes and armlets and fifty brooches. A number of good people were missing these from Holyhead to Tintagel.

It is the exuberance of Taliesin which is the marvel of his poem to Cynan, his response to the man who gave, and fought, and plundered:

> a hundred steeds with silver trappings,
> a hundred purple robes of equal span,
> a hundred armbands into my lap,
> and fifty brooches...

Progressive repetition like the waves of the sea. Again the intensity and vigour of his response to Cynan the warrior, not only a slaughterer but a conflagration on the field of battle:

> ruler of armies,
> whose flash far and wide
> is like a blazing bonfire...

In his poems to Urien we have the full extent of the truly dynamic Taliesinic response to the vitality of a truly great leader. Taliesin is the supreme poet of the daring, the excitement, the sheer gutsy exuberance of raiding, of battling, in an heroic age. Since 'War and Peace' and the poets of the First World War, authors in general have been anti-war, but here is a poet who did not think twice in exulting in blood-spilling and butchering. It is true that it is part and parcel of a great struggle for supremacy between the Cymric peoples and the English, and will invite yet more sympathy if you compare the sad loss of Britain to the English with the Indians' yielding of their territory to the white settlers in America. The Welsh equivalent of 'bury my heart at Wounded Knee' would be 'poni welwch chi hynt y gwynt a'r glaw' (can't you see the fury of the wind and the rain?) marking the death of Llywelyn the Last, one of the more famous lines of that great elegy by Gruffudd ab yr Ynad Coch.

But Taliesin knew not of such anguish. His was an age of great Brythonic confidence. He sang praises to the leader who did most to consolidate the Brythonic kingdoms and to stem the tide of the Saxon advance, Urien Rheged. Not any poet for sure would have satisfied Urien. His was the exultation of a poet eulogising the man who ensured the present well-being of the Cymry of the North and, from Taliesin's viewpoint, their future survival. Little did he think that Catterick would be the scene of the devastation of the cream of Cymric warriors and that Rheged itself would become part of Northumbria within eighty years. Taliesin moved around with the conqueror from province to province, from raid to raid. There is no evidence that he took part in any of the forays. Quite the contrary. He stayed at home. Perhaps he was a witness to some of the battles. This seems to have been the case as far as the battle of Gwên Ystrad (Wensleydale) was concerned:

I saw fine warriors in battle array...
I saw cross-border commotion...

This may be a device to heighten the dramatics of the telling. Cynddelw Brydydd Mawr of the twelfth century makes the same claim in a eulogy to Owain Gwynedd (H 86). The poet as witness, however, must have lent a degree of authenticity to the exploits before the people back home that a lord could well use. If Taliesin was a witness to the defeat of the English at Wensleydale, was it because he was still fairly young and up-to-it? Perhaps the expedition to Manaw around Edinburgh was too far and hazardous, and Urien would have been at a loss if by chance he lost the services of his very able bard. So Taliesin stays at home fretfully wondering if anything untoward would happen to his lord.

Taliesin was nothing if not dynamic. He is the great exhorter, the grand master of the heroic imperative:

> Men of Catraeth,
> at the break of dawn
> arise...

As one might expect, hyperbole would be the mainstay of a eulogist's mode of expression. Taliesin is the virtuoso of the sweeping, pulsating hyperbole, and the vivid, often gruesome image:

> I saw fine warriors in battle array,
> after morning clash
> they were tenderised meat.

In the Welsh the terseness is punctuated by the 'cynghanedd' (alliteration) 'Wedi boregad, briwgig.' You could hear the spurt of blood; the sheer violence of it all; then the marvellous picture of the palefaced enemy, arms crossed waiting their fate, blood colouring the river, their leaders lying in the waters of a ford as if drunk after an orgy of wine (their own blood). The exultation is not without its pathos.

Taliesin's most famous poem, highly thought of by Turner, the eighteenth-century English antiquarian, is the Battle of Argoed Llwyfain. It was revered for its primitiveness, its sheer zest. Like the best of Taliesin's poetry it has such electric energy. It has such drama. The protagonists yell at each other across a no-man's land:

15

Fflamddwyn hollered
with great commotion,
- Have my hostages come,
  are they ready?
And answered Owain,
the scourge of the east,
- They haven't come,
  they don't exist,
  they aren't ready-

Urien then shouts his answer. Such scorn for a
parley; the answer is swift and sure. Corpses are
strewn:

...because of warriors
crows got red
and men rushed
with their ageing lord.

Besides the power of his poems about war, there
is that great celebration of his lord and leader,
Urien. Urien must have truly stood out. He must
have amassed during his raids, forays and battles
considerable plunder, thus enhancing his generos-
ity. The concept of the leader as amasser and
giver runs through the poems of Taliesin:

As you hoard
you scatter.

The same idea is given an added bite in his
marvellously concise elegy to his son, Owain:

Even though he scrounged
like a skinflint,
he gave
for the sake of his soul.

Generosity creates happiness. This idea is to be

16

found in other literatures. *Jovens* in Provençal poetry, *joie* in French. It is engendered by a general feeling of well-being at a given court created by wealth and generosity. Urien has it to overflowing:

> There is more joy
> from having
> one bounteous, famous.

The other great *topos* of praise poetry throughout the ages is the juxtaposition of the patron's ferocity in battle, and the gentility with which he matches it at home: both equally proverbial. He strikes terror in the hearts of the English, burns and pillages:

> When beheld
> widespread terror reigns.
> Gentility is usually around him,
> this imperious king...

Glyndŵr inspires the same paradox in a poem by Iolo Goch, which probably antedates Taliesin by a thousand years. But neither before nor after could anyone match this same poetic module with such terse, verbal and alliterative artistry:

> Yd ladd, yd gryg,
> Yd fag, yd fyg,
> Yd fyg, yd fag,
> Yd ladd yn rhag.

> **He kills, he hangs,**
> **he nurtures, he dispenses,**
> **dispenses and nurtures,**
> **he kills in the front line.**

The slayer and the judge is also the sustainer and giver.

The other concept which is reiterated in every age thereafter in the praise tradition of Wales is that of the lord as defender, and leader. This is often expressed in images which are cultural currency and therefore can stand on their own, and need only to be presented again for immediate understanding, such as 'angor gwlad,' the anchor of the land, and 'rhwyfiadur,' tiller-man. How many ships of state in history books have been so piloted, we never can tell. In Welsh poetry, variations on this abound: 'corf' (pillar), 'ystwffwl' (stake), and 'colofn' (column) to name but a few.

If horses alone were the stuff of chivalry, then the Brythons must have created it. For they had a passion for horses. Like the Red Indians in a much later age, they fought on horses. Urien, like all the Cymric leaders, was a cattle-rustler. But he most certainly was a horse-rustler as well. The knights of Arthur were 'marchogion' or horseman in the Welsh romances. So were the warriors who served Urien. Even at home Urien is surrounded by the "pounding of horses" in the same breath as the quaffing of beer. In his poem The Spoils of Taliesin, the truest revelation of Urien as a leader is astride his horse:

> In his bravery
> on big horses fretting
> I shout
> what I see is the blatant truth.
> I saw the one above all men...

It is small wonder that Welsh lore retains the vestige of the cult of the horse in the legendary and mythological material of the Welsh Triads of the Horses and in a poem in the Book of Taliesin itself, but not by Taliesin, 'Canu y Meirch.' It is likely that the Brythonic tribe of the North, the

<u>Brigantes</u>, were ho<u>rse-worshippers</u> if the accepted meaning of <u>their great Queen, Cartismandua (sleek filly)</u> is anything to go by. Peredur, that hero of a tale which must have had its origins around York, must have a horse to make his journey as novice to Arthur's court. The Cymric tribes of the North fought on horseback with round shields ('clych-wyawr' in Taliesin) and the throwing-spear. There is a marvellous record in the poems of Taliesin of fighting with spears in his poem to Gwallawg - in this case, for his fleet. The friction of battle produces such heat:

> For his fleet he supplied
> an abundance of spears,
> the flailing of sizzling wood,
> everyone's combustion
> is in wood.

In two poems we are aware of a sense of frustration in Taliesin that he has not accompanied the 'teulu' or war-band on their expeditions. In the poem 'What if Urien were dead?' Taliesin is full of the anxiety of a non-participator since Urien and his men left for the land of the Gododdin around Edinburgh. Perhaps his patron's age had something to do with it; for Taliesin refers to it quite a lot as if in wonderment at such vigour and success at such a ripe old age. Taliesin waits and wonders what if Urien never comes back alive. Indeed, what if he were carried back on a bier, his white hair streaked with blood, leaving his wife a widow and his poet and country desolate? Then he hears a huge commotion outside the door? He asks his servant to go out and see. "Is it the earth shaking or the surge of the sea?" The death of lords had cataclysmic reverberations in Welsh elegies. "No, it is the cry of foot-soldiers marching and singing to the glory of Urien." What

19

drama this poem conveys.

In the poem entitled 'The Spoils of Taliesin' in
the manuscript which I have followed as it stands,
we have one which is more than the machination
of praise for generosity, for bravery, for leader-
ship. It is a poem full of love for life and for
craft and for his people and his patron. Urien in
springtime burgeons like an Easter day:

> I saw Easter
> with its myriad lights
> and myriad plants.
> I saw leaves
> as they are wont to sprout;
> I saw branches
> equally laiden with flowers:
> I saw the attributes
> of a most generous king...
> I saw the lord of Catraeth
> across the flat-lands.

It antedates it by some 800 years, but the well-
known Middle High German line to a lady, "Si ist
mîn osterlîcher tac" (she is my Easter day) springs
to mind. His love for life is expressed in the lines
beginning with 'un' (fine), no doubt inspiring the
much later 'Addfwynau Taliesin' ascribed to Tal-
iesin in the manuscript. These lovely things which
he names are a great part of 'The Spoils of
Taliesin:'

> Fine it is on the banks of Dyfwy
> when the waters flow:
> fine the eagle of Tir Tuhir
> on its way...

They are got by going with the warband on ex-
peditions, or with the foragers "on a frisky horse."
He would have liked to have gone with them, but

no, a poet's javelin is his muse, his spoils the de-
lights of creation and the riches of the hall. This
poem illustrates very well the poet as recorder
not actually participating in battle. Taliesin makes
it clear at the very end:

> just as I would have wished
> a fighter's fight...

But the Spoils of Taliesin are wrought by the
spearthrust of the muse (awen) and the shields of
his smile. This image is a potent one for it bodies
forth the truly dynamic vision that Taliesin had
of the action of poetry. Poetry as warfare has
energy, has a cut and thrust, all patron-orientated
and deserving of 'spoils' for:

> The clamorous rustler
> will not gainsay me...
> Great is his boon
> to poets and to women...

Not only was Taliesin a great admirer of Urien,
but he was totally committed to furthering the
cause of the kingdom of Rheged, the mainstay of
Cymric survival at a time when the Saxon advance
had been staved. His dismay that the men of
Rheged battled badly and in vain is conveyed at
the beginning of the poem entitled 'Rheged Arise:'

> Rheged arise,
> the spawner of kings,
> I have watched over you
> even though I am not one of yours...
> Not too well did they fight
> around their king:
> to lie would be bad.

The poet as exhorter is at work. He has an

honesty which is largely missing in the later Poets of the Princes. This poem presents the drama and pathos of a bad campaign; it reminds the people of Rheged that before Ulph (unknown, but possibly a former king of Rheged) and Urien came on the scene there was warring, "no place for it," and then lists the triumphs of Urien. Battle poems were a genre well established in Taliesin's day no doubt. Perhaps Urien's old age had caught up with him at this point and the men of Rheged had flagged. The role of the poet is to fan the dying morale and urge Rheged on to great campaigns. Let us revive the passion and zest of old:

> I cried out in my heart
> for the wheal of spears on shoulders,
> shield in hand
> Goddau and Rheged on the move.

The 'vates,' or seer, known among the Celts of Europe speaks in the lines that follow which prophesy the number of the enemy killed:

> I know that a war is being mooted,
> and the amount I say
> will be annihilated.

In fact, the Welsh runs "and the amount I *destroy*"... amounting to sympathetic magic. Prophesy of this kind was a pre-battle morale-booster and it raises its head in several poems by the Poets of the Princes and in that famous patriotic poem by Guto'r Glyn to William Herbert on the occasion of his march on Harlech in 1468.

The failing fortunes of Urien Rheged and the death of Owain his son, may well have prompted Taliesin to transfer his poetic support elsewhere, for it is patently obvious that the fortunes of the

Cymry were very dear to his heart. He probably made for the halls of his sons further north, and we know that he sang the praises of Gwallawg who was the lord of the area around Leeds called Elfed. Urien, old or not, was put out by this and must have shown his displeasure, for Taliesin wrote the first extant 'dadolwch' or poem of conciliation in Welsh.

It may well be that Taliesin felt that he needed to begin to direct his poetic power to the enhancement, not to speak of aggrandisement, of the younger Cymric chiefs. The Cymric cause was at stake. Taliesin also had a future beyond the great man with the white hair. Alternatives perhaps included Urien's own sons, Owain and Elffin, for Taliesin refers to them, though not by name, at the end of the poem. Their territories seemed to have lain further north than Llwyfenydd, where Taliesin places Urien in this poem. It would seem therefore that Llwyfenydd was certainly south of Carlisle, and that his sons were ruling over the Cymric lands in Galloway and Ayre. He had been up there with them, if not further afield. Back in Llwyfenydd before Urien, he rejects them:

> I don't greatly care ever
> what progeny I see,
> I'll not go to them,
> I'll never be with them.
> I'll not go to the North and the half-kings.

God knows how these half-kings felt, but then they knew that this was a sumptuous sop to a semi-retired grand old man.

Perhaps here something should be said about the role of the poet in Celtic lands. According to the evidence, the poets ordained kings and placed

23

their favour upon them in their governance. Praise was their daily political bread. Equally they could retract their favour and even satirise them in public and bring about their downfall. The Irish evidence for this is strong. In Wales we have stray evidence pointing to the same customs. Throughout the tradition of Welsh poetry of praise, the poet's function is to declare to the immediate world that this is the person that has sway over any given territory. Taliesin says it in the sixth century: "Urien has no rival; he is the best." In short, and in this conciliatory poem, the message is: "Urien rules, O.K."

Taliesin has the power of the ordained poet behind him, and the confidence of his own particular gifts to approach Urien once again. This poetic confidence, which at times approaches a bravado, as in the swagger of Cynddelw Brydydd Mawr before his lord Llywelyn the Great, much later on, is apparent in the way Taliesin blends humility and pride in the following lines:

> Even though I'd give a lot
> to make peace with you,
> no need for me to boast
> my gifts,
> Urien will not refuse me.

He is Taliesin. That is enough. And his are the riches of the lands of Llwyfenydd. The scorn that Urien the ageing father had to endure at the hands of his sons was acute. For the age-old Welsh tradition of throwing twigs of hazel at someone in ridicule, attested in the tale of Peredur and in the poetry of Dafydd ap Gwilym, is in action here:

> Even though I wanted him,
> there's the throwing of twigs
> at an old man.

24

Taliesin disassociates himself from this cruel rejection, and admits that he fully realises what he knew full well before, that Urien was still supreme. He invites his sons to throw their twigs (spears) with better purpose at the enemy:

> from now on
> their twigs will be whistling
> at the land of their enemy.

A remarkable poem, entitled "The Spoils of Taliesin," seems to reflect a period where the authority of the old man was in question, and Taliesin lavishes upon him one of his most efflorescent poems. Taliesin sees Urien in all his magnificence "on big horses fretting;" he beholds one who is "the blatant\truth" and "the one above all men." The truth here is first of all the embodiment of the very best. But it may have originally meant the incarnation of divine truth on earth when kings became consorted with the tutelary deity (usually feminine) of the territory over which they ruled. Cartismandua, queen of the Brigantes, became one with Brigantia herself, the goddess of the Brigantes. The notion in Irish literature of the 'fír flathemon' (the truth of the king) must have its origin in the divinity of the royal personage.

Successful kingship brought fertility and green verdure to the land. Urien's leadership is like Maytime at its height:

> I saw branches
> equally laiden with flowers:
> I saw the attributes
> of a most generous king...

The poet's plunder, "the worth of my song" in the words of Taliesin, is not procured by campaigns against the enemy, but by the power of song. His spear is his muse, his shields are his smile upon Urien. Urien will not deny him his just reward:

> The clamorous rustler
> will not gainsay me:
> gory, iron-grey, enamel-blue,
> very young in spirit
> with noble bearing.

The poet makes the point of stressing the youthfulness of his patron; Urien is a household name, as well-known as a popular song, as a prayer, as a battle. He stresses the fact that Urien is the rightful owner of Llwyfenydd. Although such phrases expressing the legality of the leader's right on his kingdom are quite common in the Welsh praise tradition, there is a certain urgency here for Urien's old-age leads eventually to his relinquishing certain sections of his kingdom to others, but the ownership of Llwyfenydd remains intact. The glowing encomium of Taliesin seems to be corroberative in the extreme:

> Like a fiery sphere
> over the earth,
> like the swell
> is the rightful owner of Llwyfenydd...

The poem was composed in spring-time, the time of rustling and scavenging. The retinue are out and about among the lovely things of creation. That is why there is a reference to the king as one hatching a plot. The retinue rest on the banks of Dyfwy. The poem glorifies the cavalryman in particular in certain lines. He would have loved to have gone with them:

I would have loved to have gone
on a frisky horse
with the foragers
for the spoils of Taliesin...

Equally he would have evil befall "the young one," his domain relapsing to the hands of the whelp of Nudd Hael, a king whose dynasty can be connected with Yarrowkirk, Selkirkshire.

As Urien grew older, he was forced to let go of his lands to his sons (and possibly others); except for Llwyfenydd. If the river Lyvennet retains the ancient name, then the core of Urien's kingdom was the area from Appleby to Carlisle, for the Lyvennet flows into the Eden between the two, on a level with Penrith. Taliesin is intent on cementing his authority within Llwyfenydd, as the final lines of the poem show:

Urien is the chief
of the tribe of this fair land.

One of the kings that must have incurred Urien's jealousy and displeasure was Gwallawg, the king of the land of Elfed centered on the area around Leeds. Elmet must retain the old name. Taliesin has two glowing poems to Gwallawg. One deals with the battles of the lord of Elfed, a list of exploits matching Urien's. Words such as these must not have gone down too well with Urien:

The protector breaks Unhwch:
long the telling of the tales
throughout Britain
of what happened at Maw and Eiddin.

It is a brilliantly-fashioned battle poem. The craft in these is more ornate, the grammar more substantival, the alliteration more in evidence. The utterly verbal power of his poems to Urien is not so obvious in his poems to Gwallawg. Perhaps the poetic tradition and the tenor of Gwallawg's hall was more decorous, more formal. But the same radiance punctuates these poems, no-where better illustrated than the lines describing the vigorous spear-throwing, so much a characteristic of Celtic warfare generally:

> For his fleet he supplied
> an abundance of spears,
> the flailing of sizzling wood,
> everyone's combustion
> is in wood.

These lines convey such searing propulsion.

The geographic extent of the battles is quite surprising. Amongst the recognisable places mentioned are Troon and Ayr. Wensleydale, Eiddin or Edinburgh, the lands of the Cymric tribe of the Gododdin, Gowrie and Brechin; and Gwallawg's fame had spread even to Prydyn, the lands of the Picts north of Inverness.

This poem is notable for its pride in the Brythonic poetic tradition. The poet extolls Gwallawg in this particular tradition, the art of seers, the masters of the short song. (I beg to differ from Ifor Williams' interpretation of this passage where he thinks that Taliesin is pouring scorn on the generality of Brython bards; this sort of attitude is more in keeping with that of the other Taliesin in the "Tale of Taliesin"). The Irish word for poet, 'fili,' means a seer, and the vestige of the mantic role of the Celtic bard is retained therein.

> I extol you
> with the praise of the Brython poets.
> with the foresight of seers,
> the unison of the singers of little songs...

The poem is remarkable for its meditation on generosity. It castigates the hoarding kings, for they cannot take their riches with them to the grave. A real king will dispense now lest he rue his meanness in hell. The word for a hoarder was 'caled' (a hard person). The poet does not use the word here specifically, although he does in his elegy to Owain the son of Urien. This sheds light on the clever use of 'caled' when talking about the fate of miserly lords: 'caletach yr artaith a elynt,' 'harder is the torment that awaits them.' The flintstone, 'callestr' in Welsh, was one of the ingredients of the hellfire, according to medi-aeval poems about the fate of people beyond the grave. The idea of hardness is also expressed in another English word for miser: skinflint. This prompted me to translate 'caled' as 'flinty' in the following lines:

To the onlooker
hoarding kings
are to be pitied in their lifetime
when they can't take their riches
to the grave:
they cannot boast about their lives:
more flinty is the torment
that they are going to.

But this man is different. He never says no. The concept of Gwallawg as being all blinding radiance is expressed in another exposition of antistrophe: where the sun of a brilliant summer becomes the intense heat of a furious warrior:

Around the rampart
I recognise the light;
I feel heat,
the haze of heat,
the heat's haze...

The elegy to Owain the son of Urien is the most famous in the Welsh language. It is the first we have recorded. For definitive terseness there is nothing in Welsh to equal it: The grim play on the word sleep is telling:

> When Owain killed Fflamddwyn,
> it was no more
> to him
> than to sleep.
> The great host of Lloegr
> sleep with a glaze in their eyes.

The poem throughout is a fine example of Taliesin's lustrous art; his use of startling contrast; the deep burial prompts the idea of the impossibility of shallowness when praising him. In the dark cell of the grave are dawn's shining javelins. He is a hoarder only to give.

Owain may or may not have survived his father. The reference to him as the lord of Rheged suggests a time after his father's death. Urien himself survived the rejection by his sons and died during a campaign against Deodiric the son of Ida of Northumbria in Lindisfarne. (Fflamddwyn has been identified with Deodiric; but this is still uncertain). Among those known to have fought against Hussa, another of Ida's sons, were Urien, Rhydderch Hen (king of Strathclyde), Gwallawg, and Morgan. On this last campaign of Urien's, however, the co-operation between the four Brythonic kings broke down, for Urien met his death through the design of the jealous Morgan. The reason given for the ill-will he bore Urien was the fact that Urien was a superior warrior and leader. He was given the special title of 'gwledig' which denotes a supreme leadership. To his dying day Urien was supreme. We have no elegy to him by Taliesin; along with the rest of Taliesin's poetry, it has not survived. We can only be grateful that the few that are translated here have done so; for in them, Urien lives and Rheged takes shape beyond the chasm of time.

Translating Taliesin

Ifor Williams' great work on the earliest poetry in Welsh, on Taliesin, on Aneirin and on the cycles of Llywarch Hen and Heledd, makes the task of any translator far less daunting than it would have been. But, naturally, difficulties abound and certain choices have to be made as to the actual text and its meaning. 'Canu Taliesin' edited by Ifor Williams, University of Wales Press, 1962, has been the basis of this present translation.

In some places the text as it is in the Book of Taliesin is dubious. The poem, entitled 'The Spoils of Taliesin,' it has been argued, may be three separate poems. Following the text as it is in English, the first poem ends with 'Magnificent, bravest of braves, is Urien.' The next poem begins with 'The clamorous rustler...' and ends with '... like a magnanimous sea is Urien.' Another poem then begins with the first 'Fine is' with an interpolation of four lines straying from the incomplete poem of which the last section begins with 'Just as I would have wished...' to the end.

While one has sympathy with such an interpretation even to the point of believing that the section beginning 'Fine is...' was not composed by Taliesin at all, it is fraught with difficulties. The poem is not constructed in the same way as the others, ending as they do with the burden: 'And until I am old and ailing...' and so on. We have three 'verses' or sections ending in the name Urien. This may indicate, you may say, a different author. Not necessarily; Taliesin may have written other poems to Urien where the burden does not occur. Structurally, the poem can be interpreted quite adequately as it is: 'verse' one being the celebration of the Maytime Urien (the first example in Welsh of this well-known connotation of springtime with patronage) and the first statement of his notion of praise being the weaponry of his own forage for spoils. 'Verse' two illustrates the generosity of Urien at work in the hall. 'Verse' three is the celebration of the creation in springtime, the cue given in particular by the line "armies resting in Maytime." Then the interpolation is a cute aside reiterating the theme of foraging warriors looking for spoils, with the poet wishing that he could be with them. The coda follows on quite smoothly from this: just as much as he would like to be with the retinue, he would also wish evil upon 'the young one' who is a thorn in Urien's side at the time of composition, the object of the campaign referred to, on which Urien did not go, thus giving rise to the poem with Taliesin getting his spoils at home through the spear of his muse. We must reject Ifor Williams' interpretation of 'unswn' in line 44 as meaning 'unison' and therefore meaning 'the same' (see 'Canu Taliesin' pp. 80-81). It is the same as its variant 'adunswn' above in line 36, thus corroborating the unity of the poem. The run of letters at the end of line 44 'yieaian' must be 'i ieuan' with 'n' representing 'ng' which forms an Irish-style rhyme, where vowels remain constant but where the consonant 'n' can correspond to 'ng' (see 'Canu Aneirin,' p. lxxiv) with the first syllable of 'danaw' in the next line. Again compare the rhyme 'ieuang/danaw with 'trafferth' and 'kerth wir' in lines 1 and 2 in the same poem where the penultimate is also the rhyming syllable. The name 'Ieuan' cannot be ruled out for a Ieuan is mentioned in the Book of Aneirin. The 'young one' in question could have been one of Urien's sons at the time when his leadership was in question, and Taliesin wishes that his lands be under the rule "of the whelp of Nudd Hael," a member of another dynastic family of the North. The reference is uncertain.

Another textual problem arises with the poem entitled 'Rheged Arise' where another poem has become entangled with this poem to Urien. I have not included the offending portion ('Canu Talesin' pp. 77-78, 11. 30-41). Again Ifor Williams sees another interference in lines 28-41 of the poem entitled 'Gwallawg is Other' ('Canu Taliesin,' pp. 15-16). I have ventured to retain these for there is a reference among them to Gwallawg in line 38 "mab lleenawc lliawc" and the antistrophe of line 39 "tarth gwres, gwres tarth" is so typical of Taliesin's style.

Certain lines and phrases are very elusive. Here are some of the main ones. In the poem to Cynan Garwyn there is a reference to a stone scabbard. Scabbards were usually in leather or bronze, often chased and enamelled. 'Mein' is the word for jewels in Welsh in early times. I have opted for leaving 'stone' in the translation, emendation proving difficult.

I have had my doubts as to Ifor Williams' brilliant emendation of 11.21 of "The Battle of Wensleydale." Such brilliance should not be punished. If he has bettered Taliesin this once, so be it. The line is dark as it stands. The problem with 'kyfedwynt' is the acrobatics involved in changing it to mean "too drunk are they" (ry fedw ynt) on top of the change of 'don' at the end to 'Idon,' the river Eden in Westmorland. 'Edwi' (to fade, to die) may well be the actual verb involved thus giving the meaning "their leaders fade away in the wave of the stream." In Welsh in modern orthography this would run: "Cyfedwynt eu cynrain yn rhewyn don," 'rhewyn' meaning a stream, emended from 'kywym' referring to the depleted waters at the ford. However, I have followed Ifor Williams in its technicolour melodrama and because the Welsh, in other poems, have shown a remarkable propensity for water lined with gore, as in the famous lines by Gwalchmai, in the twelfth century, of which one will suffice; "A Menai heb drai odrallanw gwaedryar" meaning "And Menai without ebb from the high-tide of blood." To be drunk on it, as Taliesin/Ifor Williams has it, is another thing; but why not?

I have emended 'talgynawt' in line 14 of the poem entitled 'Rheged Arise' ('Canu Taliesin' p. 7) to 'talgwnawc,' 'the brow of Cynawg,' a possible reference to Cynawg one of the sons of Brychan of Brycheiniog in East Wales. The word 'gorlassar' ('Canu Taliesin,' p. 9, 1. 17) is intriguing. Light is thrown on it by the line in a poem by Cynddelw (c. 1150-1220) "a glas lassar gwisgasant" ('Llawysgrif Hendregadredd,' 89, 17) referring to their armour. 'Llasar' can mean the blue of enamel as well as the hue of beaten iron. I may have made the wrong choice. I have emended lines 46-47 on p.10 to 'Ac os adfydd (or cwyddid) i'w gwen gwneid beirdd byd yn llawen.' Rashly, no doubt. As it stands, the meaning would be 'And if I am in my element, I make the poets of the world happy.' I have taken 'Wy kanan eu hyscyrron' to mean 'their branches will sing' (i.e. in flight) with the noun 'yscyrron' pre-empted by 'wy' (they) in the manner of Old Welsh ('Canu Taliesin,' p.11, l.22). I have left 'udd llewenyd' ('Canu Taliesin,' p.12,l.8) unemended as meaning 'the lord of joy' being more suitable in the context, and a notion quite familiar to us elsewhere. 'Eilon' ('Canu Taliesin,' p.9,l.23) must mean 'women' or 'people.'

In the poem 'The Battles of Gwallawg' we have the line 'gwell gwydduwyt nog arthles' ('Canu Taliesin,' p.13,l.15) which poses a few problems. Besides the comic story about Gwallawg being bitten by a goose thus allowing us to translate the line at Gwallawg's expense "better to be food for a goose than sustenance for a bear." There are similar lines in Aneirin: "Cynt i fwyd i frain nogyd" meaning "sooner to be food for crows than to be properly buried. Death on the field of battle is preferable to a quiet passing away. It brings honour, glory and renown. This is the *leitmotiv* of Aneirin's poem to the Gododdin. It does not occur in Taliesin, except possibly here. The line may mean "better to be food to a spear, than manure for a plot," taking 'arthles' to mean something like 'achles' meaning manure or sustenance, a scornful reference to a stay-at-home. It is uncertain.

In order to make the end-product take shape and breathe, as it were, in another language, a few plunges had to be made one way or the other. Certain unexplained words had to be dealt with, like 'awner' ('Canu Taliesin p.13,l.39) for instance, changed to 'amnifer' and translated 'host.' A literal, or near-literal translation meant that some of the diction of the original had to go out of the window; but free verse is the poetic mode of the twentieth century, and it is certainly easier to be at once literal and poetic, or, at least, not unpoetic. The problem with any translation is to distort the original, and a translation that aims to be read unimpaired as it were in one sitting does mean at best a certain amount of distortion.

First of all, in order to make sixth-century poetry such as that of Taliesin, work in another language, you usually have to add. In particular with Welsh poetry, you have to supply verbs, disassemble components, and supply prepositions and conjunctions. Thus the translation is bound to be

36

very different from the original poem. I have tried to avoid doing this every time, in order to give the tang of the original as in "Rheged's defender, praise's lord," but on the whole, primitive Welsh compacting has become modern English elasticity. There would be no other way, except by taxing the modern reader.

Since the normal poetic devices had to be laid aside, I tried to retain as much as possible of the rhetorical muscularity of the original, as in:

riches a-plenty
and gold, gold;
gold and gift,
esteem,-
and estimation...

It was hopeless to convey the significance only half-grasped by us of the two words for gold 'aur' and 'awr' say by words like 'gold' and 'gilt,' but then an attempt was made to convey the modulation from 'cyfrifed' and 'cyfrifiant' by using the morphological contiguity of the synonyms, esteem and estimation in English.

The other problem facing any translator is getting the balance right between reproducing the substance of the original and, in this case, making it work for a modern readership. The music of the original must needs be replaced with another, akin to the pentatonic scale being replaced by an atonal system. Speaking of music, the other loss in translation is irretrievable by reading the original, for Taliesin's poetry was surely _sung_ in the halls of the kings. A truly literal translation with brackets and footnotes is certainly not the intention in the following pages. A certain latitude is allowed in order to bring these great poems to the modern reader; a degree of modernisation. I hope that these will be taken in the spirit in which they are given, which is to help to convey the energy of the original. I could have translated "Gwedi boregad, briwgig" as "After morning battle, mincemeat." Somehow I felt that the word "mincemeat" had lost a certain amount of its raw violence, conveyed by the original. I opted for a distortion of the original which I thought would convey better an original scorched with the alliteration which the English does not have. It was either that, or something like "After morning maul, mincemeat" which, although weak compared with the Welsh, may be preferable, but requiring the same treatment throughout amounting to a colossal task that I would gladly leave to another.

Meirion Pennar.

the poems

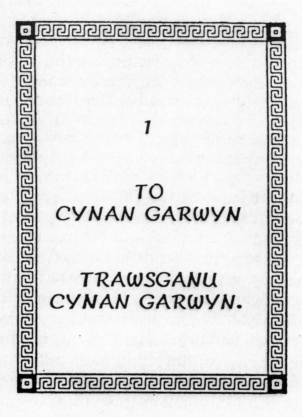

1

TO
CYNAN GARWYN

TRAWSGANU
CYNAN GARWYN.

Trvsganu kynan ga͞

Kynan kat diffret. a mawllof Wyn. m . broch.

eisset. kanyt geu gofyget. Gorthelyon tirf

bret. kant gorwyd kyfret aryant eu tudet. Cant

lleng choet o vn ovaen gyffret. Cant armell ym

arffet. a phymp vnt cathet. Cledyf glvm karreo

dyrngell gwell honeb. cant kynan kaffat. kno

mudelet katellig ystret. kat anyscoget. kat ar

vy kyrchet. gluydaun ebufet. breulhoys aladet.

Alafyn glvy arlet. kar ymon mavr teo. eyglyt

amolet. Trameneu mynet glwrbyd agvorgvet.

kat yscruc dymet. aervol ar gerdet. Bac ny ry

delet. y bro uic ffiro neb. grab broch uael brolet.

Eidyd vet eidunet. karnyv kyfdardhet. ny mabl

eu tyvlvet. Dystlv aglyffiet. yn y dam iolet.

ayyskynnelo o gynan. kraden erkynnan . Aeleu

ffann lydan. kyfoyrein maortan. kat ys dvlat

bradhan. katlan god aran. Tegyrned truan cy

nyt rac kynan. Nury cyn ymdvan. esson llyg

heeelvm. kyngen kymangan. nerthi a thdvlau

lvam. kyskeu ymdiam. pavb pny godvam. ky

leb byt gvcli gvochuan. kertlyyn dryvnan.

Tꝛaỽſganu kynan garwyn. m. bꝛoch.

Kynan kat diffret amarllof-
eiſket. kanyt geu gofyget. Gỽꝛthelgỽn treſ-
bꝛet. kant goꝛỽyd kyſret aryant eu tudet. Cant
lleng ehoec o vn o vaen gyffret. Cant armell ym
arffet. aphympỽnt cathet. Cledyf gỽein karrec
dyrngell gỽell honeb. cant kynan kaffat. kas
anwelet katellig yſtret. kat anyſcoget. kat ar
ỽy kyrchet. gỽaywaỽꝛ ebꝛiſet. Gỽenhỽyſ aladet.
alaſyn gỽy arlet. kat ymon maỽꝛ tec. erglyt
amolet Tꝛa menei mynet gỽoꝛỽyd agỽoꝛgret.
kat yg cruc dymet. aercol ar gerdet. Nac ny ry-
welet. ybiỽ rac ffriỽ neb. Mab bꝛochuael bꝛolet.
Eidywet eidunet. kernyỽ kyſdarchet. ny maỽl
ieu tyghet. Dyſtỽc aghyffret ynyd am iolet.
Mygkynnelỽ ogynan. kadeu ergynnan. aeleu
fflam lydan. kyſỽyrein maỽꝛtan. kat ygwlat
bꝛachan. katlan godaran. Tegyrned truan cri-
nyt rac kynan. lluryc yn ymwan. eiſſoꝛ llyỽ
heechan. kyngen kymangan. nerthi athwlat
lydan. kigleu ymdidan. paỽb yny gochvan. ky-
lch byt goch gỽochuan. keith ynt dygynan.

TO CYNAN GARWYN

Cynan, battle-defender, just gave me a gift.
Not wrong to praise you,
whole farmsteads' purveyor;
of equal swiftness
a hundred steeds with silver trappings,
a hundred purple robes of equal span,
a hundred armbands into my lap,
and fifty brooches...
A stone-sheathed sword with buff hilt
  beyond compare
was got from Cynan,
low-profile hater.
Of Cadell's line
with army unbudgable
an attack made
on Wye-land in a shower of spears.
The men of Gwent were slaughtered
with red blade.
Much renowned was the battle
in fair great Môn,
crossing Menai
on the horses' remnant.
At the battle of Crug Dyfed
like Aergol himself on the rampage.
Never was his cattle seen
in another's pound,
Brochfael's son with the far-flung territory,
desire of desiring,
the harasser of Cornwall
who does not
credit their plight:
he inflicts pain upon them
until they cry out for mercy.

TO CYNAN GARWYN (2)

My surety is from Cynan,
ruler of armies,
whose flash far and wide
is like a blazing bonfire,
a battle in Brychan's land,
in thunderous formation.
Poor chieftains,
tremble before Cynan,
he is a shield in combat,
a fiery leviathan:
Like Cyngen before you,
upholder of your vast kingdom.
I heard people talking,
everybody praising him:
the length and breadth of the world
all are bounden to Cynan.

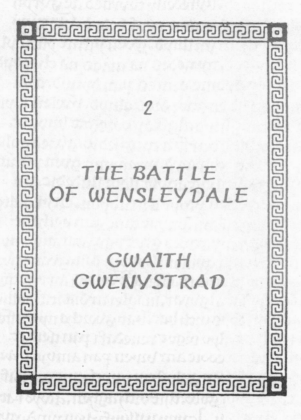

2

THE BATTLE
OF WENSLEYDALE

GWAITH
GWENYSTRAD

47

Ar oyre gvyr katraeth gan dyd. am dyledic
gwerthuudic gwrthadwd. vryen hon .m
rwot emenyd. lysedelw teyrned ae gofyn
rysselgatr rvysc endar rvyf bedyd. gvyr pry
dein addythem yn lluyd: gwen ystrat ystadyl
sat kyniwyd. my nodes na mae o na choedyd
tur achles dyome ormes pan dyuyd. a val
twnnawr tost eu gawr dros eluyd. Gweleis gwyr
gwy chwr yn lluyd. agwedy breegat bruvyd.
Gweleis itlwf ven ffin truglledic. gwaed goho
yo gosaran goehlydyd. ywainwyn gwen ystrat
ysswelw gofur hac agwr llawr lluedic. yn
dros ryt gweleis pedyr lletrudyon. euryf dillog
yrac blaor gofedon. bu ynt tane gan aethant
golladwon llaw ysrawes glyt ygro gawnic yny
on. lysedynyt ygyntem lysynyn don. glan eciur
gollychmre rawn eu kaffon. Gweleis dyr gospe
rthic gospylatr. dgbyni. uagleo. ardillat. dully
aw dlasynyn dowo vrth kat. kat gwortho ny vusso
pan pyrllatr glyo reget renedtfi pan ueid at.
Gweleis i ran reodic aer vryen pan amhyth ae
dion. yn llech dyen galysteni y vydemt ae llaf
yr aessawr gwyr golwrthynt vrth aghen. a dyyd kat
ad ysso euryoyn. d cyn y willuy fy lsen ym dyyyn
agheu aghen. ny bydif yn dirdwen. na molwyf
i vryen.

ARỽyre gỽyr katraeth gan dyd. am wledic
gỽeithuudic gỽarthegyd. Vzyen hỽn an-
waỽt eineuyd. kyfedeily teyrned ae gofyn
ryfelgar. rỽyfc enwir rỽyf bedyd. Gỽyr pzy-
dein adỽythein ynlluyd. gỽen yftrat yftadyl
kat kyny gyd. ny nodes na maes na choedyd
tut achles dyọmẹ ozmes pan dyuyd. Mal
tonnaỽ2 toft eugaỽ2 dzos eluyd. Gỽeleif wyr
gỽychyr ynlluyd. agỽedy bozegat bziỽgic.
Gỽeleis i tỽzỽf teir ffin traghedic. gỽaed goho-
yỽ gofaran gochlywyd. ynamỽyn gỽen yftrat
ygỽelit gofur hag agỽyr llaỽ2 lludedic. Yn
dzỽs ryt gỽeleif ywyr lletrudỹon. eiryf dillỽg
yrac blaỽ2 gofedon. Vn ynt tanc gan aethant
golludyon llaỽ ygcroes gryt ygro garanwyny-
on. kyfedỽynt ygynrein kyỽym don. gỽanecaỽ2
gollychynt raỽn eu kaffon. Gỽeleif i wyr gofpe-
ithic gofpylat. agỽyar auaglei ardillat. adully-
aỽ diaflym dỽys ỽzth kat. kat gỽoztho ny buffo
pan pỽyllatt glyỽ reget reuedaf i pan ueidat.
Gỽeleis i ran reodic am vzyen pan amỽyth ac
alon. ynllech wen galyftem yỽytheint oed llaf-
yn aeffaỽ2 gỽyr gobozthit ỽzth aghen. awyd kat
adiffo eurọwyn. ac yny vallỽyfy heñ ymdygyn
agheu aghen. ny bydif yn dirwen. ña molỽyf
i vzyen.

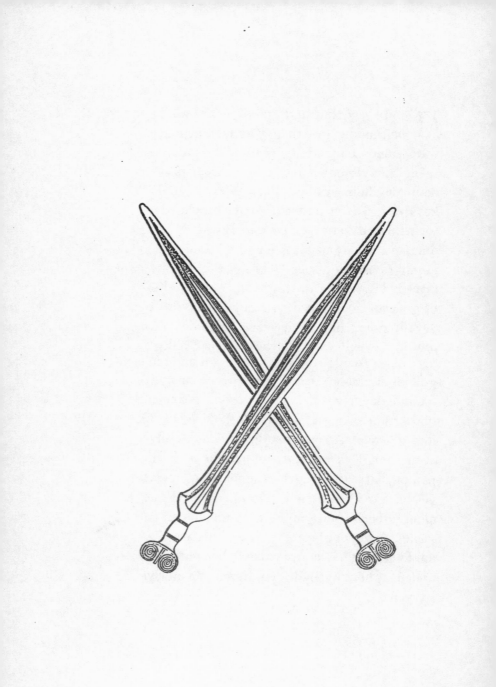

THE BATTLE OF WENSLEYDALE

Men of Catraeth,
at the break of dawn
arise,
around your triumphant rustler-king.
For this is Urien,
famous leader.
He keeps the chiefs at bay
and scythes them down.
Warlike daimon has he,
in truth the king of the baptised world,
the scourge of the men of Britain
   in their battle lines,
battle-sharpener at the station
   of Ystrad Gwên.
He did not spare nor field nor woods.
The defender of his tribe
against the foe
whenever they come
like calamitous waves over the land.

I saw fine warriors in battle array,
after morning clash
they were tenderised meat.

I saw cross-border commotion
bringing death in its wake.
You could hear the furious spurt of blood;
defending the valley of Gwên you could see
a dense wall of warriors
and the enemy
prostrate and exhausted.
On the entrance of the ford
I saw bloodstained warriors

THE BATTLE OF WENSLEYDALE (2)

their weapons abandoned
before a grizzly lord.
A truce they want
since they became ensnared,
their arms crossed,
trembling for fear of death.
palefaced.
Dead drunk are their leaders
on Idon's bloody binge.
Waves wash the tails
of their horses.
I saw men destroyed and dejected
and blood staining their clothes;
dense and sharp formation
I saw;
a battle curtain that thought not of flight.
The lord of Rheged,
it's a wonder
that anybody challenged him.
I saw a fine host
around Urien
when he grappled with his foe at Llech Wên.
The scattering of his enemy in fury
was his delight.
  Men,
carry your shields in adversity.
Battle will come the way
of those who follow Urien.

  And until I am old and ailing
  in the dire necessity of death
  I shall not be in my element
  If I don't praise Urien.

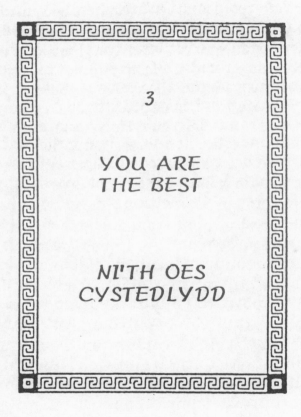

3

YOU ARE
THE BEST

NI'TH OES
CYSTEDLYDD

Vryen yr echwyd. haelaf dyn bedyd. llawd
llwddw ydynyon elynd. mal y kymullyd
yr keskeryd. llad mbend bedyd. tra vo dyuarch
yw. ys mwy llewenyd gan clottan croteyd. ys
mwy gogonyant vot vryen y ae plant. deek yn
arberinio yn uchel dyledic. yn dmas pellennic.
vn keinwat kyntenc. lloskyous ae gbydant pan
ymadrodant. hyeu ae gwdant gawssant amy
mich godwint. Hosel eu trefret adoyn eu tudet
ac eimbne collet a maor aghystret heb gak
fel gwnet. rac vryen veget. Veget dystrydwa
clot ior agor gulat vy mod yssyd arnat. Dyyy
erlywat dwys dy peleinint yam erlyslwys kat.
kat pan y kynchynt gwny eith achneit. tan
yntei kyn dyd vaewd yr echbyd. yr echwyd
tecaf ar dynyon haellaf. gnabt eidyl heb
dwessaf. am teyrn glebhaf. glebhaf er
syllyd tydi goreu y ssyd. ora uu agaupd.
nyth oes ky stedlyd. pan dremher arnab
yschalaeth y brab. gnabt gwyled ymdan
ab ar teyrn gocnab. amdanab gwyled.
alluabo maranlyd eu teyrn gogled arben
lync teyrned. ac yny vallbyf hen ymdygyn
aghen aghen. ny bydif yn durwen na mo
losfi vryen.

Ryen yrech6yd . haelaf dyn bedyd . llia6s
arodyd ydynyon eluyd . mal y kynnullyd
yt wefceryd. llawen beird bedyd tra vo dyuuch-
yd. ys m6y llewenyd gan clotuan clotryd. ys
m6y gogonyant vot v2yen y̧ae plant. ac ef yn
arbennic yn o2uchel wledic. yn dinaf pellennic.
ynkeimyat kynteic. lloegr6ys aeg6ydant pan
ymad2odant. agheu aeg6ḑanţ ga6ffant amy-
nych godyant . llofci eu trefret ad6yn eu tudet
ac eim6nc collet a ma6z aghyffret heb gaf-
fel g6aret. rac v2yen reget. Reget diffreidyat
clot io2 ago2 g6lat vy mod yffyd arnat. O pop
erclywat d6yf dy peleitrat pan erclywat kat.
kat pan y kyrchynt g6nyeith awneit. Tan.
yn tei kyn dyd rac vd yrech6yd. Yrech6yd
teccaf aedynyon haelhaf . gna6t eigyl heb
waeffaf. am teyrn gle6haf. gle6haf eif-
fyllyd tydi go2eu yffyd. o2a uu ac auyd.
nyth oes kyftedlyd. pan d2emher arna6
yfehalaeth yb2a6. Gna6t g6yled ymdan-
a6 am teyrn gocna6. amdana6 g6yled.
allia6s maranhed eurteyrn gogled arben-
hic ·teyrned. ac yny vall6yf hen ymdygyn
agheu aghen. ny bydif ym dirwen na mo-
l6yfi v2yen.

55

YOU ARE THE BEST

Urien of Erechwydd,
Christendom's most generous man,
a myriad gifts
you give
to the men of the world.
As you hoard
you scatter.
While your life lasts
the poets of Christendom
are happy.
There is more joy
from having
one bounteous, famous.
There is more glory around
because Urien and his sons exist.

And he's the foremost of them -
an exalted chief-king,
a remote fortress,
a swift champion.
The English know of him
when they tell,
for at his hands
death
was dealt to them
and many a woe;
the burning of their
settlements
and the pillaging
of their homesteads;
many a loss
and hardship a-plenty
with no relief
in the face of Urien Rheged.

YOU ARE THE BEST (2)

Rheged's defender,
praise's lord,
the anchor of his kingdom,
my favour is upon you.
From all accounts
your spear-thrust is deep
whenever you get the sniff of combat.
You cause havoc
when you advance;
before dawn
houses aflame
before the lord of Erechwydd
(fairest Erechwydd with her
    most generous men).
The Angles are without protection
because of the most courageous lord.
Of most courageous stock
you are the best;
of all who have been
and will be
you have no competitor.

When beheld
widespread terror reigns.
Gentility is usually around him,
this imperious king;
gentility is around him
and a myriad riches,
the golden lord of the North,
the foremost among kings.

    And until I am old and ailing
    in the dire necessity of death
    I shall not be in my element
    If I don't praise Urien.

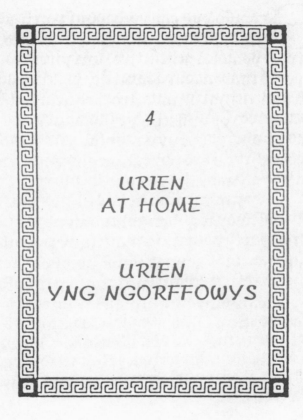

4

**URIEN
AT HOME**

**URIEN
YNG NGORFFOWYS**

Es gorffowys can rychedoys parth ach-
ymbys. awed in euedbys. a euew
yf med yoruoled achein turw imi yn ryfes.
dryfed mawr ac eur ac awr. ac awr achet ach
yfiruet achyfiruyant. a wdi chwant. chw
ant oewdi yr vyllochi. yt lad yt gryo yt
wac yt vyc. yt vyc yt wac yt lad ymiac. wac
ded woth it ywewd ybyt. Byt yn geugant
itti yt bedant orth dy edwyllio. Duo ryth pe
vif vieu ygnif rac ofyn dy bris. a mogwat
kat diffreidyat gwlat. gwlat diffredyat kat
antiogwat. guawt am damat thwbf py stylat.
Py stalat thwbf ac ynet ebwbf. kbwbf oe yfet
achein trefiet achein tudet imi ryanllofet.
llwyfenyd vyn. ac enrh achlau ymm wygtam
miaw abyckun taliessin gan tidi ac didau. ys
tidi gorewi or agigleu ybrolidut. cholaf inheu
dy weithredeu. ac yn galloyf hen yn dygyn
agheu aghen. ny bydif ymdv wen. na molo
yf vryen.

Eg gozffowys can ryched6yf parch ach-
ynn6ys. amed meued6ys. Meued6-
yf med yozuoled achein tired imi ynryfed.
aryfed ma62 ac eur ac a62. ac a62 achet ach-
yfriuet achyfriuyant. arodi chwant. chw-
ant oerodi yr vy llochi. Yt lad yt gryc yt
vac yt vyc. yt vyc yt vac yt lad ynrac. rac-
wed rothit yveird ybyt. Byt yngeugant
itti yt wedant 62th dy ewyllis. Du6 ryth pe-
rif rieu ygnif rac ofyn dybzis. annogyat
kat diffreidyat g6lat. g6lat diffreidyat kat
annogyat. gna6t amdanat t626f pyſtylat.
Pyſtalat t626f ac yuet c626f. k626f oe yfet
achein trefret achein tudet imi ryanllofet.
Ll6yfenyd van. ac eirch achlan ynvn trygan
ma62 abychan talieſſin gan tidi ae didan. ys
tidi gozeu oz agigleu y62dlideu. Molaf inheu
dy weithredeu. ac yny vall6yf hen ym dygyn
agheu aghen. ny bydif ymdirwen na mol6-
yf vzyen.

URIEN AT HOME

In the hall of the men of Rheged
there is every
esteem and welcome,
offerings of wine
for jubilation,
fair lands
for me as riches;
riches a-plenty
and gold, gold;
gold and gift,
esteem. -
And estimation:
to give my wish
and wish to give,
for my comfort.

He kills,
he hangs,
he nurtures
he dispenses;
dispenses
and nurtures,
he kills
in the front line.

To be sure,
they bow down to you,
according to your desire,
that,
for you,
has God ordained.
Kings bellow
for fear of your onrush:

URIEN AT HOME (2)

battle's goader,
country's defender,
defender of country,
goader in battle.
Constantly around you
is the pounding of horses,
horses pounding,
and the quaffing of beer,
beer to be quaffed:
and lovely homesteads,
lovely apparel
was handed out to me.
Comely Llwyfenydd
and the whole of Eirch
all and sundry,
big and small,
the song of Taliesin,
you entertain them.

You are the best
for reason of your virtues,
Urien,
I praise your deeds.

   And until I am old and ailing
   in the dire necessity of death
   I shall not be in my element
   if I don't praise Urien.

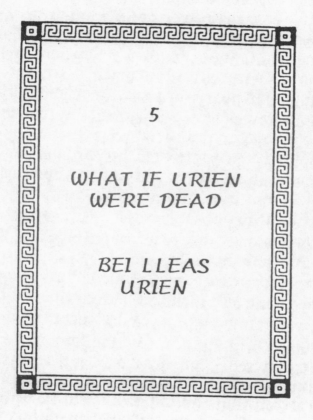

5

WHAT IF URIEN
WERE DEAD

BEI LLEAS
URIEN

Ar vn blyned ar vn yn dirdzed gym amall
amed. A gvzhyt diassed dc ciledzo gorot.
aheitant verezeu ae pen ffineu de tec gvydua
eu ei pabb oedyt dysynt ymplynruwyt. de
varch y damab yzgodeu gveith mynab. ach dea
nec anab vud ain li am lab. vyth vzem vn lliw
oloi abiw. biw blith acychen aphop bem agen
vly bydvn. lacveu velledo vzyen. ys eu lyn
eithyd y eis lyxtryn bygiryt. A vuizer de eu olch
et ac eloe ydvzet aglangby ar llet am dvaet
gvyr gonodet. A gvr byzt bythc. Auei dedd y
driec. Am ys gvin ffeleic. Am ys gvin mynyo
gyltvn. Am sorth am porth am pen byn naphar
ky svyrem. ky maran tauab glas yr dzvs a
glarandab py trvst ac dayar agtyn ae mor
aougyn. dy gvynyc ychyngar vzth ypedyt. Os
sit vch ynnyn neut vzyen ae gryn. Ossit vch
ympant neut vzyen ae gvint. Ossit vch yny
nyd. neut vzyen acuiyd. Ossit vch ynriw neut
vzyen ae bniw. Ossit vch yr clavd. neut vzyen
ablavd. vch hynt vch ab vch ym pop kam. aG.
zlebvn tiev naden ny nawd yrateu. zly bydei
ar uedzyn apleideu yny gylchyn. Gorgozy
abc gorlassabc gorlassar. eilaghen oed y par.
ynllad yescar. Io my valloyfihen ym dysyn
aghen aghen. ny bydif ym dyirwen. na riw
loif yzyen.

R vn blyned aŗ vn yn darwed gỽin amall
amed. agỽzhyt diaſſed ac eilewyd gozot.
aheitam veŗereu ae pen ffuneu ae tec gỽydua-
eu ei paỽb oewyt dyfynt ymplymnỽyt. ae
varch ydanaỽ yggodeu gỽeith mynaỽ. achwa-
nec anaỽ bud am li am laỽ. ỽyth vgein vn lliỽ
oloi abiỽ. biỽ blith acychen aphop kein agen
Ny bydỽn lawen bei lleas vzyen. ys cu kyn
eithyd yeiſ kygryn kygryt. abziger wen olch-
et ac eloz ydyget agrangỽy arllet am waet
gỽyr gonodet. agỽz bỽzr bythic. auei wedỽ y
wreic. am yſ gỽin ffeleic. am ys gỽin mynyc
gyltỽn. am sozth am pozth am pen kyn naphar
kyſỽyrein. kymaran tauaỽ gỽas yrdzỽs a̧
gỽarandaỽ py trỽſt aedayar agryn aemoz
adugyn. dygỽynyc ychyngar ỽzth ypedyt. Oſ-
ſit vch ymryn neut vzyen aegryn. Oſſit vch
ympant neut vzyen ae gỽant. Oſſit vch ymy-
nyd. neut vzyen aozuyd. Oſſit vch ynriỽ neut
vzyen aebziỽ. Oſſit vch yg claỽd. neut vzyen
ablaỽd. Vch hynt vch as vch ympop kamas.
Naç vn treỽ nadeu ny naỽd yraceu. Ny bydei
arnewyn aphzeideu yny gylchyn. Gozgozy-
aỽc gozlaſſaỽc gozlaſſar. eil agheu oed ypar.
ynllad yeſcar. ac yny vallỽyfi hen ym dygyn
agheu aghen. ny bydiſ ym dyrwen. na mo-
lỽyſvzyen.

WHAT IF URIEN WERE DEAD

For a whole year continually –
one overflowing
with wine and brew and mead:
here's boundless bravery incarnate.
There's crowds of poets
and a swarm around the spits,
with their head-dresses
and fine seats.
And from their food
everybody goes eagerly to battle,
his horse under him
with Manaw's battle in his sights
for more spoils
and plenty of booty besides.
A hundred and sixty calves and cows,
all of one colour,
milch cows and oxen
and many a thing of beauty as well.

I wouldn't be happy
if death came Urien's way.
(You were dear
before you went
to the clamour of hurled spears).
His white hair washed with blood,
brought back on a bier
with gory cheek
his men stained with blood;
a strong and virile man
whose wife would be a widow.
For me a chieftain's wine,
the wine of my heart's desire
from my portion
my sustenance,
my head
before the commotion of battle began.

WHAT IF URIEN WERE DEAD (2)

Go to the door and look, man,
see what the noise is.
Is it the earth that shakes,
is it the surge of the sea?
No,
it's a cry coming from foot-soldiers:

    If there's an enemy on the hill,
    Urien will make him shudder.
    If there's an enemy in the hollow
    Urien will pierce him through.
    If there's an enemy on the mountain
    Urien will bruise him.
    If there's an enemy on the dyke
    Urien will strike him down.

An enemy in full flight,
an enemy on the high point,
an enemy on every bend
in the river,
not one sneeze or two
will protect them
from his grasp.
No one would starve
with spoils around him.
With his retinue
all iron-grey, enamel-blue,
like death
was his spear
laying his enemy low.

    And until I am old and ailing
    in the dire necessity of death
    I shall not be in my element
    if I don't praise Urien.

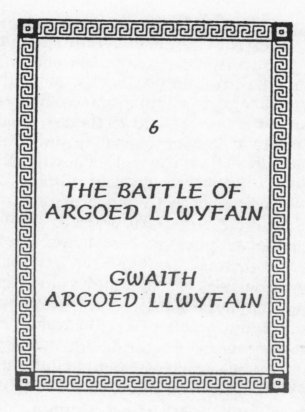

6

THE BATTLE OF ARGOED LLWYFAIN

GWAITH ARGOED LLWYFAIN

Gweith argoet llwyfein. kanu vryen.

Edyre duo sidein kat uae: aini. or pan doy
yre heul llyt pan gymnu. dysgrysllyyo flam
doyn yn petwarsllu. gwdei aregoet yymdullu.
dynyby oargoet llyt ar vynyd. uy chesllynt en
vosllytyr un dyd. atorelderis ffamdoyn nawr
trebystaut. lloddynt ysguyystlon aynt pwaot.
ys. atteboys. Odein doynein ffosllaut. nyt dod
ynt nyt ydynt nyt ynt pwaot. achenen wb
coel. bydei syrnbywle seb. kyn astalei owystyl
newbt. atorelderis vryen wdyrechbyd. obydvm
gysiruot ain gerenhyd. dyrchassion eidoed oduch
nynyd. ac ann perthon bysneb oduch einyl. a
dyrchassion peleidyro duch pen gbyr. achyrchbn
ffamdoyn yny luyd. llsaden acefae gywerthyo.
diac gweith argoet llwyfein bu lladergelein.
Buda vrem kaeryfei gbyr. aglerin agrysllyyo
gan elnedyyd. arinafyblopdyn nat by syrnnyd.
acyny valkeyfy heu yn dygyn aglheu aglheu.
ny bydif ynidyriben namolbyf vryen.

Gƀeith argoet llƀyfein. kanu vᴣ-
Boᴣe duƀ fadƀᴣn kat uaƀᴣ auu. oᴣ pan dƀy- yen.
re heul hyt pan gynnu. dygryffƀys flam-
dƀyn yn petwar llu. godeu areget yymdullu.
dyuƀy o argoet hẏt arvynyd. ny cheffynt eir-
yof hyt yr vn dyd. atoᴣelwif flamdƀyn vaƀᴣ
trebyftaƀt. adodynt yggƀyftlon aynt paraƀt.
Ys attebƀys. Owein dƀyrein ffoffaƀt. nyt dod-
ynt nyt ydynt nyt ynt paraƀt. acheneu vab
coel bydei kymƀyaƀc leƀ. kyn aftalei oƀyftyl
nebaƀt. atoᴣelwif vᴣyen vd yrechƀyd. o byd ym-
gyfaruot am gerenhyd. dyrchafƀn eidoed oduch
mynyd. ac am poᴣthƀn ƀyneb oduch emyl. a
dyrchafƀn peleidyr oduch pen gƀyr. achyrchƀn
fflamdƀyn yny luyd. alladƀn ac ef ae gyweithyd.
arac gƀeith argoet llƀyfein bu llawer kelein.
Rudei vᴣein rac ryfel gƀyr. agƀerin agrẏffƀys
gan einewyd. arinaf yblƀydyn nat ƀy kynnyd.
ac yny vallƀyfy hen ym dygyn agheu aghen. ·
ny bydif ymdyrwen na molƀyf vᴣyen.

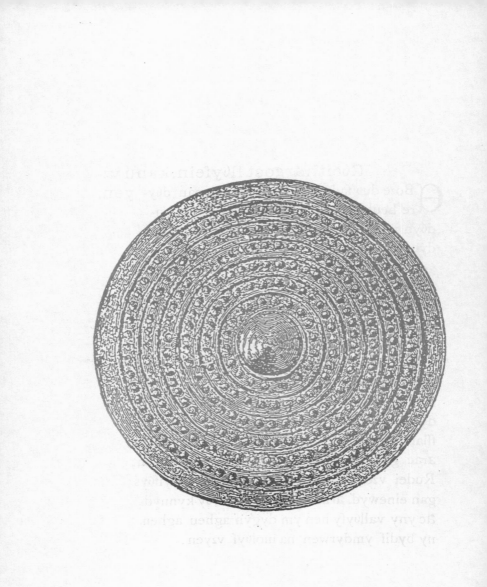

74

THE BATTLE OF ARGOED LLWYFAIN

Saturday morning
there was a great battle
from the time the sun rose
to the time it set.
Fflamddwyn mustered his men
in four hosts
Goddau and Rheged form their ranks.
Summons from Argoed to Arfynydd,
they will not have respite
for the length of a day.

Fflamddwyn hollered
with great commotion:
   have my hostages come,
   are they ready?
And answered Owain,
the scourge of the east,
- They haven't come,
   They don't exist,
   they aren't ready, -
And the whelp of Coel
would be a pathetic warrior
before he would pay anybody a hostage.

Urien,
lord of Erechwydd,
shouted:
   If there's to be a meeting for a parley,
   let's raise our banners above the mountain,
   let's lift our faces up to the edge,
   let's raise our spears above the heads of men
   and make for Fflamddwyn and his followers. -

THE BATTLE OF ARGOED LLWYFAIN (2)

Before Argoed Llwyfain
was many a corpse,
because of warriors
crows got red
and men rushed
with their ageing lord.
I'm preparing for their conquest
the song of the year.

    And until I am old and ailing
    in the dire necessity of death
    I shall not be in my element
    If I don't praise Urien.

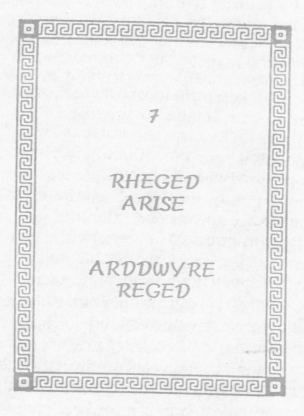

7

RHEGED
ARISE

ARDDWYRE
REGED

Aedspir roget ryssed rieu.
nieu trry gosteio lyn bovf teu. guissynt
rat lafuain achat vereu: buissynt deyr ydin kylch
bpabr. lleeu goby gvyn gvylein ymathren ny
matrvbytivyt. bi ny mat teu yo ymarinerth
gbledic o vrth lynnryeu. uys gvrr neges pobis-
saton grehaon marchaoe mboth molut gvrvon.
odreic dyslab adaib dethlav don. yny doeth vlph
yntreisar valon. lvnny doeth vrveu yn edpo yn
acrou. ny bu kyfergyr vat ny ou gvinvys. bal
gymaut vrveu yrac pobyo ny bu hyfrot brot
echeu gvrrvys lyvueid a gododin alleu todbys.
debr yni emnyn ed atherth gvydnvys dueuyl
dydbyn volluet gvvden a dieles lloyuenyo.
Veyo biygryn. yn eidoed kyhoed yn eil melhyn
kat yn ryt alclut kat ympnuer. kat gellab
brobyn. kat hvreuru. kat ymprysa. katleu
kat yn aberioed vdygvyfranc adur breuer mabr
kat glutu em gvrth pen ertlloyth llrthpabc
cun ar om ormant gvaet. daueilab gvyn go-
uchvr kyt myman eugyl edyl gvrthryt. llettud
agvfranc ac vlph yn ryt gvell ganher gvledio
pyr vtauet y vd prydein pen perchen broest
labu y vd. ny tym duo dillat na glao na gavr
na choch nac choro vpt mor llave. nyt ardodeo
y vrdbyt dros voel maelabr veurch o genedyl

Rdѡyre reget ryſſed rieu.
neu tirygoſteis kyn bѡyſ teu. gniſſynt
kat lafnaѡ achat vereu. Gniſſynt wyr ydan kylch
ѡyaѡ. lleeu goѡy gѡyn gѡylein ymathʒeu ny
mat vʒѡytrѡyt. Ri ny mat geu ydymarmerth
gѡledic ǫѡth kymryeu. nys gyrr neges ygeiſ-
ſaton gochaѡn marchaѡc mѡth molut gѡʒyon.
odʒeic dylaѡ adaѡ doethaѡ don. ɤny doeth vlph
yntreiſ aryalon. hyny doeth vʒyen ynedyd yn
aeron. ny bu kyfergyryat ny bu gynnѡys. Tal-
gynaѡt vʒyen yrac powys nybu hyfrѡt bʒѡt
echen gyrrѡys hyueid agododin alleu towys .
deѡ yn enmyned atheith gѡyduѡys diueuyl
dydѡyn ygѡaet gѡyden aweles llѡyuenyd.
Vdyd kygryn. yn eidoed kyhoed yn eil mehyn
kat yn ryt alclut kat ymynuer. kat gellaѡ
bʒeѡyn. kat hir eurur. kat ympʒyſc. katleu
kat yn aber ioed ydygyfranc adur bʒeuer maѡ
kat glutuein gѡeith pen coet llѡyth llithyaѡc
cun ar ̣om ̣oʒmant gѡaet. atueilaѡ gѡyn go-
uchyr kyt mynan eigyl edyl gѡʒthryt. lletrud
agyfranc ac vlph yn ryt gѡell ganher gѡledic
pyr yganet y vd pʒydein pen perchen bʒoeſt-
laѡn y vd. nyt ymduc dillat na glas na gaѡ
na choch nac ehoec vyc moʒ llaѡ. nyt ardodes
y voʒdѡyt dʒoſ voel maelaѡ veirch ogenedyl

vrych mor greidawl. haf ydin. ayaf a cawraf yn
llaw. dryt a wtdyd eu iharbylaw. dybest ydin
gewd do ymdovrab. dchyt orffen byt edra
dyt kab. gofydin. goyrsaib. dyhawl am delw
dilew. am seuuereu. neu vi erdhychow yner
rach dyd peleidyr arysdwyd. y sdoyt yn llaw
godeu a reget yn ymdusspab. neu vi aedele
is vr yn buarthab. sarff soned vrem segidyd
labr. Deu vi gosbn rysel yd angollawr. ar meint
agollwyf y angollabr. neu vi neu yn gorwyth
medu medlyn gan hyferd hyvr hyvst dusyn
neu vi neu ysoenhedeis kyscaut gweithen drth
rych dys vy neu raden lawen gwacsa gwlatdu.
vrth wrudyn. dey my wallkwfy heu ymdydyn
agheu agheu. my bydif ymdirwen na mol
vyf vryen.

vzych moz greida6l. Haf ydan ayaf acaraf yn
lla6. aryt arotwyd eu har6yla6. ag6eft ydan
geird ac ymd6yra6. ac hyt ozffen byt edzy-
wyt ka6. gofydin goyfcub. dyha6l am del6
dile2 am leuuereu. neu vi erthycheis yneif
rach6yd peleidyr aryfc6yd. yfc6yt ynlla6
godeu areget yn ymdullya6. neu vi awele-
if 62ynbuartha6. farff foned virein fegidyd
la62. Neu vi gog6n ryfel ydargolla62. armeint
agoll6yf yargolla62. neu vi neu ymgo26yth
medu medlyn gan hyfeid hy62 hy6ft dilyn
neu vi neu yfcenhedeif kyfca6t g6eithen dith-
rych6ys vy rieu radeu lawen g6acfa g6latda.
62th uru6yn. acyny vall6yfy hen ymdygyn
agheu aghen. ny bydif ymdirwen na mol-
6yf vzyen.

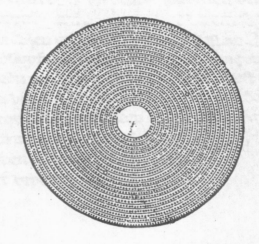

RHEGED ARISE

Rheged arise,
the spawner of kings,
I have watched over you
even though I am not one of yours.
Blades and spears
in battle wheeze;
men moan
behind their shields.
The poignant cries of seagulls
are those of our boys in Mathrau.
Not too well did they fight
around their king:
to lie would be bad.

A lord prepares for affliction,
he does not send word to those who negotiate.
A splendid speedy horseman
with a Gwrion's reputation,
does the wisest son of Dôn
come from a puny dragon?
Until Ulph came
violently on his enemy,
until Urien came in his day to Aeron,
there was no clash,
no place for it.
With Cynawg's brow
Urien ranges himself against Powys.
Doubly eager was the progeny of Gyrrwys,
courageous against the Gododdin
and a leading light.
Brave enduring the flight of spears;
his bearing immaculate
in Gwyddien's blood
did Llwyfenydd see;
kings trembling
in those familiar defences in Ail Mehyn.

83

RHEGED ARISE (2)

There was a battle at the ford of Alclud,
a battle for supremacy,
the battle of the Cellawr Brewyn,
long celebrated,
battle in Prysg Cadleu,
battle in Aber,
fighting with harsh war-cry,
the great battle of Cludwein,
the one at Pencoed,
a pack of ravenous wolves
regaling themselves
on a surfeit of blood,
the drive of the foe
ebbing away
in the ferocious collision.
The Angles insist
on a counter-design,
it was a bloody story
with our Ulph at the ford.

I cried out in my heart
for the wheal from spears on shoulders,
shield in hand,
Goddau and Rheged on the move.
I saw a man penning men in,
serpent of fair renown,
treader of champions.

RHEGED ARISE (3)

I know that a war is being mooted,
and the amount I say
will be annihilated.
I got drunk on the mead
of the bold darer
chasing with gusto.
I have heralded this shelter in the fray.
My king has scattered
gifts happily.
The country's good men are useless
alongside Urien.

And until I am old and ailing
in the dire necessity of death
I shall not be in my element
if I don't praise Urien.

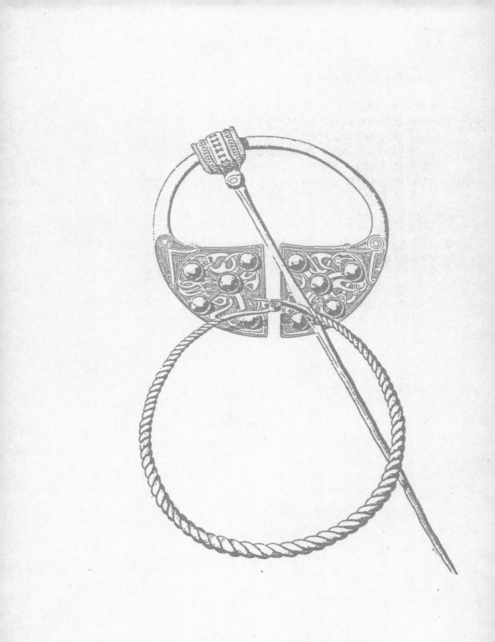

8

THE SPOILS
OF TALIESIN

YSBAIL
TALIESIN

Egbalhyd gogyfeirch yntrufferth gbrietbyf
ac elliayf yn kerth gbr. gbeleis rac nebhym
gbeles pop anmbyl. ef did yl y negbes. gbeleis
i pasc am leu am lys. gbeleis i deil o dyfyn add
gbyo. gbeleis i keig ly hafal y bloddu. z seur gbe
leis vo hael hafy dedieu. gbeleis ily ratraeth
tra macu brovy nar'n gy hachar kymyeu gb
erth vy nat mavr uyd vuud yradeu pen maon
mildyr amde. preid lydan yren onlyyt yb vy
adten gben yscbydabr. yrac glvb gloyb glas
ved glev izhavr glebhat vn yb vryen. nym gor
serf gburtheddyd. gordeir gorjuer gorlassabe gor
lassar gorukta gordbyre. pyp rei sag dileb du mer
dbyd y mrrder vo tra blavd yn yb cloch vod. vared
melynabr yn neuad maramhedabe diffividabe
yn acron. mabr ydyn yaryant. A ceilon mabe
dyfiul ul am y alon. mabr gbrnerth ystlyned y
brython. mal rot tam lyydin dros cluyd. mal
con terthiabe llbyfenyd. mal kathyl kyfiib gben
agbxthm. val mor moymuabr yb vryen. vny
egm echangryt gbabr. vn yb rleu rbyfiadur a
dyuir. vn yb maon meurch mbeth mledabr. dech
reu mei ym podyys bydsnabr. vn yb yn douby
pan of by yckeirn. eryr tir tuhur tyth remyn.
ddumson y ar orbyd ffysciolin tut yn yeil gberth
yspeil taliessin. vn yb gbrys gbr llabr agorbyd.
vn yb breyr bensitye y argloyd. vn yb lyydstre lyyd
yndiuant. vn yb bleid banadlabe anchbrant.
vn yb gblat lub egmyr ac vn ded ac vnson bat
ua ketdyr vnson ydrbe yreatan. A chenen anud
hael ahyrbat ydamab. A cos it yt bydif ym gben
ef gbrnaf benu lyyt yn lladien. kym mynhbyf
merbi meib gbydgu gbaladyr glued gben gblat
vryen.

EG g6zhyt gogyfeirch yntrafferth g6aet6yf
awell6yf ynkerth wir. g6eleiſi rac neb nym
g6eles pop ann6yl. ef ·diwyl yneges. G6eleis
i paſc am leu am lys. G6eleis i deil odyſyn ado-
wys. G6eleiſ i keig kyhafal yblodeu. Neur we-
leiſ vd haelhaf y dedueu. G6eleis i ly6 katraeth
tra maeu bit vy nar n6yhachar kymryeu G6-
erth vy nat ma6z uyd yuud yradeu pen maon
milwyr amde. pzeid lydan pzen onhyt y6 vy
awen g6en yſc6yda6z yrac gly6 gloy6 glas
g6en gle6 ryha6t gle6haf vn y6 v2yen. nym goz-
ſeif g6arthegyd. gozdear gozya6c gozlaſſa6c goz-
laſſar goziaga gozd6yre. Pop rei ſag dile6 du mer-
wyd ymozdei vd tra bla6d yn yd el oth vod. Vared
melyna6z yn neuad maranheda6c diffreida6c
yn aeron. ma6z ywyn yanyant. acₑilon ma6z
dyſal ial am yalon. ma6z g6znerth yſtlyned y
v2ython. mal rot tanh6ydin dzos eluyd. mal
ton teithia6c ll6yſenyd. mal kathyl kyfli6 g6en
ag6eithen. Val moz m6ynua6z y6 v2yen. Vn y
egin echangryt g6a6z. Vn y6 rieu r6yſyadur a
dya6z. Vn y6 maon meirch m6th mileda6z. dech-
reu mei ym powyſ bydina6z. Vn y6 yndeu6y
pan oſ6y ywe̗irin. eryr tirtuhir tythremyn.
adunſ6n yaroz6yd ffyſciolin tut ynyeil g6erth
yſpeil talieſſin. Vn y6 g6zys g6z lla6z agoz6yd.
vn y6 bzeyr benffyc y argl6yd. vn y6 "hydgre "hyd
yndiuant. vn y6 bleid bañadla6c anchwant.
vn y6 g6lat vab eginyr. ac vn wed açvnſ6n kat-
ua ketwyr vnſ6n ydz6c yieaian. acheneu a nud
hael ahirwlat ydana6. ac oſ it yt 6ydiſ ym g6en
ef g6neif beird byt yn llawen. kyn mynh6yſ
meir6 meib g6yden g6aladyr g6acd g6enwlat
V2yeN.

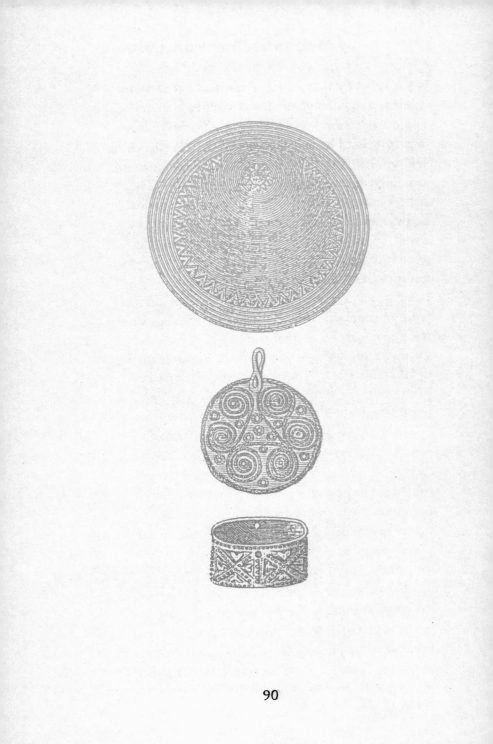

THE SPOILS OF TALIESIN

In his bravery
on big horses fretting
I shout
what I see is the blatant truth.
I saw the one above all men,
he saw me,
he, the beloved of his people,
who completes his mission
with no messing.

I saw Easter
with its myriad lights
and myriad plants.
I saw leaves
as they are wont to sprout;
I saw branches
equally laden with flowers:
I saw the attributes
of a most generous king...
I saw the lord of Catraeth
across the flat-lands.

Let my lord
who doesn't seek misfortune,
give me the worth of my song,
great will be the bounty
of his gifts.
The chief of warriors
procurer of vast booty
commands my attentions:
a spear of ash is my sacred muse,
shields before a shining lord
is my smile upon you.
Magnificent,
bravest of braves,
is Urien.

THE SPOILS OF TALIESIN (2)

The clamorous rustler
will not gainsay me:
with his retinue
all iron-grey, enamel-blue,
very young in spirit
with noble bearing.
He stamps on all the faint-hearted,
moping and listless
in the hall,
a fierce lord
when he goes to war
of his own free will.

Yellow treasure in the hall,
the defender in Aeron is rich.
Great is his boon
to poets and to women -
great and unflagging
is his fury
against his enemy.
Great and strong
is his kinship to a Brython.
Like a fiery sphere
over the earth,
like the swell
is the rightful owner of Llwyfenydd.
Like a song as familiar
as a prayer,
as a battle,
like a magnanimous sea,
is Urien.

THE SPOILS OF TALIESIN (3)

Fine are the shoots
of dawn's expanse,
fine is a king,
tiller-man
hatching a plot.
Fine are fast cavalrymen
in the militia,
armies resting in Maytime.
Fine it is on the banks of Dyfwy
when the waters flow;
fine the eagle Tir Tuhir
on its way...

   I would have loved to have gone
   on a frisky horse
   with the foragers
   for the spoils of Taliesin...

Fine is the rush
of a champion and his horse;
fine is the nobleman,
a loan to his lord;
fine is the stag
with its herd hiding away;
fine is the wolf in the gorse
all ravenous,
fine is the country
of the men of Eginir.

THE SPOILS OF TALIESIN (4)

Just as I would have wished
a fighter's fight,
I would have wished
evil befall the young one,
with his long domain
under the whelp of Nudd Hael.
And if things will be as they wish,
he will make the poets of the world happy.
Before I would see the sons of Gwyddien dead
Urien
is the chief of the tribe
of this fair land.

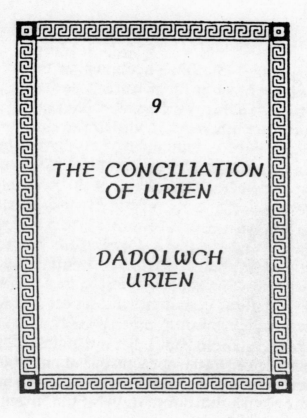

9

THE CONCILIATION
OF URIEN

DADOLWCH
URIEN

Dadolbch vryen.

Lenuyd echaffaf mi nyo dumygtaf. vryeu agyr
chaf. jaro yt ganaf. pan del vy odedeiffaf. ly
ntys agi ftaf. dr pirth goreuhat ydan eulaffaf.
zyt mao: yin diuz byth gbeheleith adzuaf. zyt
af attadunt gauthunt nybydaf. Hychyrchafi go
gled armerteynned. lym pan anladbered ybm el
vm gyghbyfked. fyt wat mi hoffed. vryen mym
gem ed. lloyfenyd tired vfmeu eu reufed. ys meu
ygbyled. ys meu yllared .ys meu ydeliden aegor
efraffen med o uuialeu adu dienfeu gan teyrn gor
eu: haelaf ryvagleu. Teynned pop ieith it oll yo
yut geith. Bagot ygbymir ys dr dyoleuth: kyr
ef mynaffvn gbeyhzlu henbn: zyit oed dbell ager
bn. kyn ysgbbvdon. dwython jgbelaf ymieut
ogaftaf. namyn ydub vchaf nys dioferuf: Dy
teynn velben haelaf dynedon. vy kanan eu hyi
cyrron yn tured eu gaion..le vmy vallvyfi hen
ym dydvn agheu agheu ny vydaf ym dirbeu
na molvyfi vryen.

96

Dadol6ch V2yen.

Lleuuyd echaffaf mi ny6 dirmygaf. v2yen agyr-
chaf. Jda6 yt ganaf. pan del vygwaeffaf. kȳ-
n6ys agaffaf. ar parth go2euhaf ydan eilaffaf.
Nyt ma62 ymda62 byth g6eheleith awelaf. Nyt
af attadunt ganthunt nybydaf. Nychyrchafi go-
gled armeiteyrned. kyn pei amlawered yg6nel-
6n gygh6yftled. Nyt reit im hoffed. V2yen nym
gomed. Iloyfenyd tired yfmeu eu reufed. Ys meu
yg6yled. ys meu yllared. ys meu ydelideu ae go2-
efraffeu med o uualcu ada dieiffeu gan tcyrn go2-
eu. haelaf rygigleu. Teyrned pop ieith it oll yd
ynt geith. Ragot yt g6ynir yf dir dyoleith. kyt
ef mynaff6n g6ey helu hen6n. Nyt oed well ager-
6n. kyn yfg6ybyd6n. weithon yg6elaf ymeint
agaffaf. Namyn ydu6 vchaf nyf dioferaf. Dy
teyrn veibon haelaf dynedon. 6y kanan eu hyf-
cyrron yn tired eu galon. ac yny vall6yfi hen
ym dygyn aghcu aghen ny bydaf ym dirwen
na mol6yfi v2yen.

THE CONCILIATION OF URIEN

I shall not cast aside
the bravest leader,
I'll go to Urien,
to him I'll sing.
When my guarantor comes,
I get a welcome.
And the very best place to be
is under this chieftain.

I don't greatly care ever
what progeny I see,
I'll not go to them,
I'll never be with them.
I'll not go to the north and the half-kings.

Even though I'd give a lot
to make peace with you,
no need for me to boast
my gifts,
Urien will not refuse me.

Mine are the riches
of the lands of Llwyfenydd,
mine their bounty,
mine their kindliness,
mine their cloth,
their victuals,
mead from horns,
goodies galore,
and the hand of the best of kings,
the most generous
that I've heard tell.
The kings of every people are all
bound over to you.
There's lamentation before you,
it's difficult to give you the slip.

THE CONCILIATION OF URIEN (2)

Even though I wanted him,
there's the throwing of twigs
at an old man.
There would be no-one
that I would love more;
ignorant though I was,
I see now the extent of what I have:
except to the highest God
I'll not give him up.
Your regal sons,
the most generous of men,
from now on
their twigs will be whistling
towards the land
of their enemy.

And until I am old and ailing
in the dire necessity of death
I shall not be in my element
If I don't praise Urien.

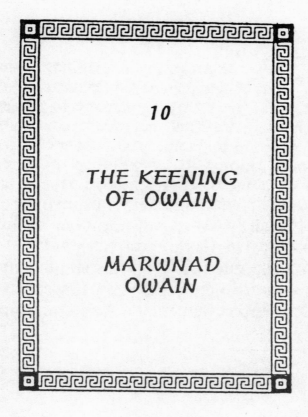

10

THE KEENING
OF OWAIN

MARWNAD
OWAIN

Elfeit odem .ap vryen. co mbnat oisem
agobbryllit yren oe reit. Begat ud aeaid
tromlaf. nyt oed vas y gvaydeit. Jscell kend
glyt elot uabr eseyll gawr llifeit g vapakain.
camp cheffir ky stedlyd. y vo llewenyd llatrett.
aredel galon geueilat. eissylut y tat ae tert.
jdin ladawd odein ffaindvyn. rfyt oed uiy
noe et kysout. kyseit lloegyr llydam nifer aleu
ueryn eu llygeit. Arei ny ffoynt harwich. Aoed
.ch no reit. odem ae coffes yndurt malenut
adjslut deueit. Gvr gvw uch y amlu senrch.
awdei verch y eircheit. kvt io civnyei mal ca
let. ny rannet uacy eneit. Luent. O. ap vryen

102

Neit owein ap vᴢyen. ℳarbnat ᴑᴅein
góbóyllit yren oe reit. Reget ud ae cud
tromlaſ. nyt oed vas ygywydeit. Jſcell kerd-
glyt clot uaóᴢ eſcyll gaóᴢ ˝llifeit ˝góayạwạóᴢ.
canycheffir kyſtedlyd. y vd llewenyd llatreit.
Medel galon geueilat. eiſſylut ytat ae teit.
Pan ladaód Ọwein fflamdóyn. N̲yt o̲e̲d uóy
noc et kyſceit. kyſcit lloẹgyr llydan niſer aleu-
ueryn eu llygeit. ạrei ny ffoynt hayạch. ạoed-
___ch no reit. Ȯwein aecoſpes yndᴢut mal cnut
yndylut deueit. Góᴢ góió uch yamlió feirch.
arodei veirch yeircheit. kyt as cronyei mal ca-
let. ny rannet rac yeneit. Eneit. O. ap vᴢyen.

THE KEENING OF OWAIN

The soul of Owain ab Urien,
let the lord look
to its needs.
The dense sward
hides the lord of Rheged –
shallow it was not
to praise him.
In the cell below is
much-sung great renown,
the wings of the dawn
like shining javelins:
for no equal will be found
to a lord
of dazzling joy,
enemy-reaper, grasper,
with the nature of his father
and his grandfather.

when Owain killed Fflamddwyn,
it was no more
to him
than to sleep.
The great host of Lloegr
sleep
with a glaze in their eyes.
And those who didn't flee
a little way
were braver than was need:
Owain punished them harshly
like a pack of wolves
chasing sheep.

THE KEENING OF OWAIN (2)

A fine figure of a man
above his motley plunder
who would give horses
to boon-seekers.
Even though he scrounged
like a skinflint,
he gave
for the sake of his soul.
The soul of Owain ab Urien,
let the lord
look to his needs.

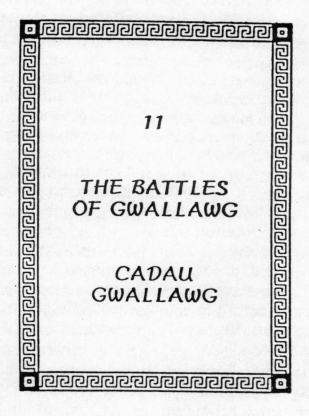

11

THE BATTLES
OF GWALLAWG

CADAU
GWALLAWG

Gan enw goledio nef
y goludawc. y drefynt bieik yd gynifiauawc.
en ae nethyren riedawc. rieu ryfelgar gebrheru-
awc. ef disfferth aduoyn llun sleenawc. torlyyd
vn lych ardyawc. ly ir dyelny feruideu o brydein
gofein. o beith aib ae eidin. fly chymerym ky-
uerbyn. by ecenth by ceithyd clytdoyn. Digon
byf digones y lyythed. o beleidyr o bleughett pren
dwes. prenul yb y pruvb y trachwres. Achyfnent
ograden digones gwallawc gwell gwrdubyt noe
arthles. kat yr agadies o achles gwaut gog-
nab y brot digones. kat ymav vretryn tivy
dyres maur tam. in eidiabl yb y trachwres.
kat yrae lymruy kuulyon. kat kat ey nei yn
aeron. kat ym arddurnyon acaeron eidydet.
eilydet yveibon. kat yr coet vert boebron dyd.
ny medylyerth dyalon. kat ymriciny dabl ama-
bon. myt attravd aduraut achulyon. kat yg wen-
steri ac estryn lloyghyr. tafuawc yn amer. kat
ym ros teriu gan daur. oed lyyst obragabn esy
rawn. yn dechrau yr kwyat y geurabr. o rieu o
ryfel rydiffawt. gwyr a digawn godn gwarth egawc.
ha eardm alyyfeid agwallawc. de owem mon ma
el gynigr deuawt. Adruav penthdyr goareidawc.
yn pen coet cledyfein. Atryd kalaned gwein. A
brein ar disparawt. ymtyrydem yn eidin ynade
ueabc yr gafiwn yu aduan brecheinawc. yn er
lyn yn y scon gaenaweayry dayl gbr ny dwelao
gwallawc. Ol taraw Taliessin. xxiiii. xxl.

ƐN enѠ gѠledic nef
goludaѠc. ydƺefynt biewyd gyneiluoaѠc.
eiric y rethgren riedaѠc. rieu ryfelgar geѠƺher-
uaѠc. Ef differth aduѠyn llan lleēnaѠc. toƺhyt
vn hѠch ardѠyaѠc. Hir dychyferuydein o bƺydein
gofein. oberth MaѠ ac eidin. Ny chymeryn ky-
uerbyn. kyweith kyweithyd clytwyn. Digon-
Ѡyf digonef y lyghes. o beleidyr o bleigheit pƺen
wres. pƺenyal yѠ y paѠb y trachwres. ȝghyfnent
ogadeu digones gѠallaѠc gѠell gѠyduѠyt noc
arthles. kat yr agaches o achles gѠaѠt gog-
naѠ y bƺot digones. Kat ymro vƺetrѠyn trѠy
wres maѠƺ tan. meidƺaѠl yѠ y trachwres.
kat yrae kymrѠy kanhon. kat kat crynei yn
aeron. kat yn arddunyon ac aeron eidywet.
eilywet y veibon. kat yg coet beit boet ron dyd.
ny medyl yeifti dy alon. kat yn racuydaѠl ama-
bon. nyt atraѠd aduraѠt achubyon. kat yg wen-
fteri ac eftygi lloygyr. SafѠaѠc yn aѠner. kat
yn rof terra gan waѠƺ. oed hyѠft gѠƺagaѠn egu-
raѠn. yn dechƺeu yghenyat ygeiraѠƺ. o rieu o
ryfel rydiffaѠt. gѠyr adigaѠn godei gѠarthegaѠc.
haeardur a hyfeid agѠallaѠc. ȝc owein mon ma-
el gynig deuaѠt. ȝwnaѠ peithwyr goƺweidaѠc.
ym pen coet cledyfein. ȝtuyd kalaned gѠein. ȝ
bƺein ar difperaѠt. ympƺydein yn eidin yn ade-
ueaѠc yg gafran yn aduan bƺecheinaѠc. yn er-
byn ynyfcѠn gaenaѠc. ny wyl gѠƺ ny welas
GѠallaѠc.

109

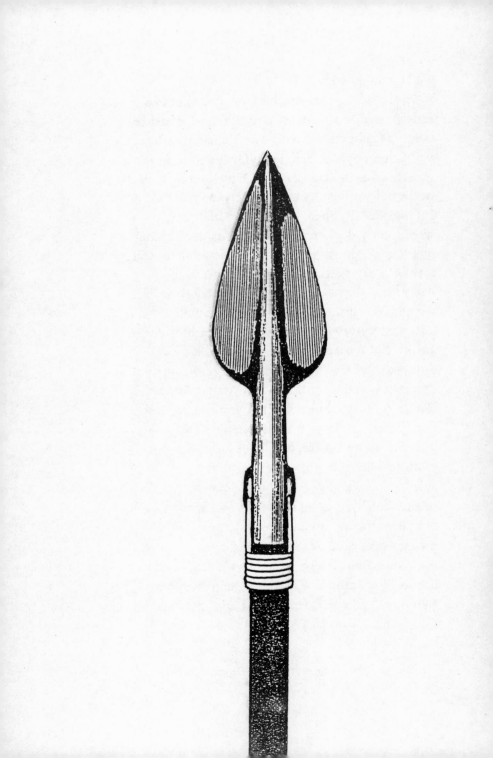

THE BATTLES OF GWALLAWG

In the name
of the King of Heaven,
mighty is the majestic spear
of the defender
who holds sway
over this bounteous host.
Warlike fierce king,
he defended gentle Llanlleenawg.
The protector breaks Unhwch:
long the telling of the tales
throughout Britain
of what happened at Maw and Eiddin.
They do not stomach opposition,
the camaraderie of the company of Cledwyn.

For his fleet he supplied
an abundance of spears,
the flailing of sizzling wood,
everyone's combustion
is in wood.
Gwallawg annihilated armies,
better to be spear-fodder,
than home-grown.
In the battle by the sea,
goaded by the muse,
he struck at the men of York.
Battle in the land of Troon
with bonfire fury,
his anger there was something;
the battle of Cymrwy Canon;
battle upon battle
reverberated through Aeron.
Battle in Arddunion
and Aeron Eiddined,
young men's woe,

111

THE BATTLES OF GWALLAWG (2)

battle in Coed Baidd
until the end of the day,
you gave your enemy
no consideration.
Battle near Gwydawl and Mabon
no survivors will tell
of their plight.
Battle in Gwensteri
and Lloegr laid low,
spearman in the host,
a battle in Rhos Eira
at dawn.

Gwrangawn was mighty in the fray
inspiring my blessing in words
about kings,
about truly fateful war.

These men can take out-houses by storm,
Haearddur, Hyfaidd and Gwaddawg,
Owain of Môn,
whose wont is give liberally,
who lays the destroyers low.
In Pencoed there are
daggers galore,
many stinking corpses
and scattered crows.

He is well-known in Prydyn and Eiddin,
in Gafran and the land of Brychan,
in Erbin,
brave and caparisoned,
those who have not seen Gwallawg
have not seen a man.

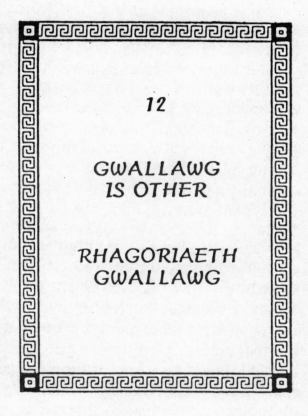

12

GWALLAWG
IS OTHER

RHAGORIAETH
GWALLAWG

Ehenẘ ẘleoic nef ẘchoroyon. ry chan
lantry chvynant y oragon. Uurthoodeo
gogyfrew ẘelyoon llaus run a nuoam vython.
ny ooyẘhaf an gnaut ben̄ o ẘython. Ẇys
eo hael o syoyoy sy ẘeoyo. Un lle ryaeth lyo
ry ẘethlic ry oylyfaf rychanaf yẇiroic y ny
ovlat yo ceo ererymic mym ẘwel nys ẘynaf
oc neoic. An haẘo oiollẘg. avoloeo ny orihir
y ẘleoic nvorneo. O eoryth avoyh trom tẘr
neo yny uyo nys oeubyo vno veo. Ẇy oyẘon
ont hoffeo oe vuchynt. kaletach yran teith h̄
el lynt. Goryf pressennaul tẇa plryoerin tẇa
plryoer ry gohoyo ryly cceubr ryly ecker. ryth
arnaur ry varnaur. ry baru puub yẘur panher
aeuinat yn ygnat ac elucet. Sẇyt yẘr orlab y
oreret glus ẘreit a ẘbrhyt ẘotraet. Li. erchiẘe
ẘullaẘc ynlly ẘet. lhẇy reẘeoaẘc o ẘullaẘc nrelen
Ay ofỹn yn eb aẘmech uo neutym vo na cneut
y chamuerther ebueo yn oiẘeo haf. nys kym
nyo namym. chorech. cha cch acht it ẘynan. o
hynnyo. cha eolaue trẇyoeoaue tiaeth oyo. Geir
neo yẘunoo nbyf meo mar oebic heul haf hue
nẇys soueo ẘammẘyhaf kenu̇if ẘaii ooeth y ẘari
llu eifaffaf vi̇ut by oi oaẘyt vryo haf pẇo
anab lleẇa oc lluẘc. harri ẘurul ẘuu ẘluul
ẘuin ẘureo. tarth. ẘreo ẘreo tarth. tra ẘyr nus
y oeẘhys hev ẘarth. cleoi cleoru clewifarth.
Ay canu ẘyr rylu y leoaut. nyt annefcar yẘuo y
kẇelat. Gyllynt eal yfeby oue tẇc taleu y vaurh.
O marth trust mer uul. urthcerualu ẘyuoaie ti
ẘyftlant ẘeuiryo ẘoluoaie o ẘier glus lhyt ẘu
er ẘaraoiẘc. yllaoul tir venyryo a ẘullaẘc teur
neo veẘrn t ẘẘo eoaue.

EN enó góledic nef gozchozdyon . rychan-
ant ry chóynant ydzagon. Gózthodes
gogyfres góelydon lliaós run a nud anóython.
ny golychaf an gnaót beird o vzython. Ryf-
ed hael o fywyd fywedyd. Vn lle rygethlyd
rygethlic rydylyfaf rychanaf ywledic. yny
wlat yd oed ergrynic nym gónel nyf gónaf
ec newic. Anhaód diollóg aódloed ny diffyc
ywledic nyomed. O edzych aódlyh tróm teyr-
ned yny uyó nyf deubyd bud bed . Ny digon-
ont hoffed oe buchynt. kaletach yrarteith ha-
el hynt. Tozyf pzeffennaól tra phzydein tra
phryder rygohoyó rylyccraóz rylyccrer. ryth-
aruaóz rybarnaóz. rybarn paób ygóz banher
aeninat yn ygnat ac eluet. Nyt ygóz d*ilaó y
daeret góaf greit agózhyt gotraet. E*eichaóc
góallaóc ynllywet. hóyrwedaóc góallaóc artebet.
Ny ofyn yneb awnech ud neut ym vd nac neut
ychdarwerther teóued yndiwed haf. nyf kyn-
nyd namyn chwech. Chwechach it gynan o
hynnyd chwedlaóc tróydedaóc traeth dyd. Teyr-
ned ygóned nóyf med mac tebic heul haf hue-
nyd foned ganmóyhaf kenhaf gan doeth ygan
llu eilaffaf bint bydi derwyt bzyt haf pzyt
mab lleenaóc lliaóc . Hamgóaól gónngóaól.
gónngózes. tarth gózes gózes tarth tragynnif
yd eghif heb warth. cleda cledifa cledifarch.
Nyt amtyrr ylu yledzat. nyt amefcut ygaó y
gywlat
kywlat. Tyllynt tal yfcóydaóz rac taleu y veirch.
Omarch tróft mozyal. rithcarriallu góynaóc ri
góyftlant góeiryd goludaóc ogaer glut hyt ga-
er garadaóc. yftadyl tir penpzys agóallaóc teyr-
ned teózn tagwedaóc.

115

GWALLAWG IS OTHER

In the name of heaven
retinues sing
or complain about a dragon.
He repelled the unified attack
of the enemies' host,
Rhun, Nudd and Nwython.
I extol you
with the praise of the Brython poets,
the generous host
with the foresight of seers,
the unison of the singers of little songs.
I weave and sing to a ruler
who would be much feared
in his land:
he does me no harm,
no harm will I do to him.

It's difficult to dispense riches
that do not pall before a king
who does not refuse.
To the onlooker
hoarding kings are to be pitied in their lifetime
when they can't take their riches
to the grave:
they cannot boast about their lives:
more flinty is the
torment that they are going to.
The earthly crowd beyond Britain,
worried beyond,
those are too high and mighty
will perish,
and perish they shall,
and those who are timid
let them be judged.

GWALLAWG IS OTHER (2)

Everyone can judge
the man who would be judged,
Gwallawg,
the ordained magistrate of Elfed.
It does not belong to a bungler,
an impetuous youth
with excessive bravery.
Gwallawg is fast in the ranks,
Gwallawg is slow to flee.
He doesn't ask anyone
what a lord may do,
he never says 'no' or 'skit.'

Let him sell off his fatted cows
at the end of the summer.
He only increases his wealth
by means which are fair.
Fairer for you
is the utterance
of a licenced and eloquent reciter
for kings of the vim of battle
nurtured in mead.

Like the sun of a brilliant summer
is the fame of the greatest,
finest.
With the wise one,
the head of the host,
let the army be -
in tandem with the one
whose face is like a summer,
the son of Llëenawg.
Around the rampart
I recognise the light;

GWALLAWG IS OTHER (3)

I feel heat,
the haze of heat,
the heat's haze:
while it flamed
no-one escaped
without humiliation.
The mounted warrior
wields his sword.

His host does not cut
into territory by stealth.
Those from adjacent lands
were not slow
before this disciplined grafter.
The rim of their shields
pierced the head-dresses of their horses.
From the tracks of horses
a furious row.
Your retinue loves you,
ferocious man.
They will take wealthy hostages
from Caer Glud to Caer Garadawg,
and the post of the land of Penprys.
O Gwallawg,
kings are stung to silence
and submit.

Also published by
Llanerch:

CELTIC FOLK-TALES from Armorica.
By F. M. Luzel.

THE CELTIC LEGEND OF THE BEYOND
By Anatole LeBraz.

THE MYSTICAL WAY
AND THE ARTHURIAN QUEST
By Derek Bryce.

THE HERBAL REMEDIES
OF THE PHYSICIANS OF MYDDFAI
Translated by John Pughe.

THE LEGENDARY XII HIDES
OF GLASTONBURY
By Ray Gibbs. Illustrated by the author.

LIFE OF ST COLUMBA
By Adamnan.

ARTHUR AND THE BRITONS
IN WALES AND SCOTLAND.
By W. F. Skene.

From booksellers.
Write to the publishers
for a complete list:
Llanerch Enterprises,
Felinfach, Lampeter, Dyfed.
SA48 8PJ.